GREAT CARS

VOLKSWAGEN
BEETLE

GREAT CARS

VOLKSWAGEN
BEETLE

A celebration of the world's most popular car

RICHARD COPPING

Published by Veloce Publishing Ltd, Veloce House, Parkway Farm Business Park, Middle Farm Way, Poundbury, Dorchester, Dorset, DT1 3AR

Tel: 01305 260068 Fax: 01305 250479
E-mail: info@veloce.co.uk
Website: www.veloce.co.uk

Printed and bound in India by Replika Press

PHOTOGRAPH CREDITS

All archive pictures copyright Volkswagen Alktiengesellschaft apart from:
Porsche Werksfoto 10/11

All archive pictures sourced from Volkswagen Alktiengesellschaft apart from:
Author's collection: 6, 7, 8, 9, 13 bottom right, 17, 18, 19 top, 22, 27, 31, 32, 37, 39 bottom, 43, 47, 49, 50, 51, 58 top, 59, 61, 62 right, 64, 66, 67 bottom, 68/69, 71, 72, 73, 74, 75, 77 top right, 83, 86 top right, bottom left and right, 87 top right, 89, 95, 96, 97, 99, 102, 103 bottom, 104, 105 top middle and right, 106, 107, 111, 112 top, 113, 114 top, 115, 116/117, 118, 119, 120, 121, 122, 124, 125, 126, 128, 129, 130, 131, 132, 133, 134 top left and right, 136, 137, 138, 139 bottom, 147, 148, 149 middle, bottom left and right, 151, 152, 160/161, 162, 163, 168, 169, 170 left, 171 bottom right.
Brian Screaton collection: 62 left

Studio photography by John Colley: cover, 52–57, 78–82, 90–94, 142–146, 154–159

Contents

INTRODUCTION

The Volkswagen Beetle: undoubtedly the most instantly recognisable and nameable car of all time, unquestionably the most written about automobile in the world, and certainly the most prolific in gross number; no contemporary manufacturer came anywhere near to producing in excess of 21.5 million cars of a single type, and – despite the more recent spurious claims of both Toyota and VW themselves that a string of vehicles bearing the same name qualify – it remains highly unlikely that anyone will ever deliberately set about the task of toppling the Beetle's unique record.

That so many Beetles were built and that its tentacles extended across the world is down to one man, Heinrich or Heinz Nordhoff, Volkswagen's first post-war director general and a giant in motor manufacturing circles throughout the 1950s and 1960s. Why Wolfsburg's resident kingmaker decreed that the vehicle he had decided to champion must be available across the entire alphabet of countries is reasonably easy to ascertain; but why, as an experienced player in the automobile industry, Nordhoff chose to cling to one model as the lifeblood of his business for in excess of 20 years, and in the process defy the laws of motor manufacturing, has to be a topic of immense interest in any celebratory volume concerning the iconic Beetle.

Similarly, the story behind the Beetle's creation in the first place invites careful scrutiny, and its true parentage has to be unveiled however unpalatable that

truth might be. Beetle inventor Ferdinand Porsche's track record of failure to push plans for a small car for the largely un-motorised German people of the late 1920s and early 1930s past the early prototype stage suggests that the relative ease of the Beetle's progress from concept to production – epitomised in the building of a factory for its manufacture – was the work of an external force of both considerable power and persuasive influence. Only those blind and deaf to the horrors of the Second World War of 1939 to 1945 could fail to recognise the role that

Right: Volkswagen's PR department ensured that a steady flow of images of director general Nordhoff and his beloved car were available. This one dates from the early 1960s.

the Nazi government of pre-war Germany, under its despotic leader Adolf Hitler, played in the Beetle's creation.

Likewise, while Nordhoff surely revelled in the glory of being the Beetle's adoptive father, the role of another man who fostered the car's well-being for little more than a transitory period following the rightful annihilation of its mentor cannot be overlooked. Had this British officer done no more than he was asked to do by his superiors, when he descended upon the battered and bruised former works built originally for the sole purpose of producing Beetles, there might well have been no car for Nordhoff to champion.

The greatest debate of all occurs when analysing the period in the Beetle's story after Nordhoff's death in April 1968. Historians generally, and the corporate history department at Wolfsburg particularly, trot out the old line that the Beetle had reached its sell-by date, and that by relying on it for too long the Volkswagen empire was almost brought to its knees in an engulfing tide of debt. Such a story, once perhaps conceived as a necessary ploy to market the Beetle's successor – the redoubtable Golf or the somewhat tainted Rabbit – is no longer entirely plausible. Now is the time to scotch such propaganda, just as firmly

as the politically and socially apt line that Ferdinand Porsche alone created the great car. Beetle production broke new records after Nordhoff's death; the key American market's love affair with the Bug held firm. Four years of management incompetence at Wolfsburg followed by an economic crisis of a then unprecedented scale brought Volkswagen to the brink of disaster, not the Beetle. Once eclipsed in Germany, the Beetle became or remained the mainstay of Volkswagen's prosperity in both Brazil and Mexico, where in the latter country at least it would survive until the early years of the present century.

Below: Retired roadworthy Beetles were often put to a whole host of new uses. In this instance a car has become a farmer's workhorse, providing straight and narrow ploughing services with first gear engaged and no more than 15kph behind the speedometer needle. And the message? Old Beetles don't wear out, they're just reallocated to new tasks.

Above: For the best part of two decades and in excess of 160,000 kilometres the specially-built Beetle train acted as chauffeur to over 130,000 visitors to the Wolfsburg factory. The former home of the Schulenburg family, Castle Wolfsburg, is visible in the background.

Fascinating though this untangled and re-knitted story of growth – from tainted interloper to both world player and icon of the age for a 30-year period before relative but long-lasting obscurity in a South American retreat – might be to any historian, and informative to even the most casual of readers, it cannot be overlooked that this is not a mere history book, but a volume dedicated to a great car, the Volkswagen Beetle. With or without a soft top; built within Wolfsburg's hallowed portals or assembled, possibly even manufactured, in far-flung corners of the world; offering a candle of six-volt electrics, the challenge of a lack of synchromesh, and conceivably the scary inefficiency of cable brakes; breaking with the tradition of Beetle benchmark torsion-bar technology in favour of conventional Macpherson struts; with a panoramically curved windscreen and a modern moulded plastic dashboard; or latterly with fuel injection in the best tradition of modern technology – it's the car that calls the tune.

At the heart of every Beetle was the famous flat-four air-cooled engine, generating no more than a maximum of 50PS over 40 years after it was conceived, but still loved the world over for its honest simplicity and enduring longevity. This above all was what made the Beetle great, a rightful claimant the accolade of car of the 20th century and justified bearer of the title *Der Weltmeister*.

Acknowledgements

It might appear strange to start with thanks to someone who is no longer with us, but without the intervention of Ivan Hirst, Senior Resident Officer at Wolfsburg in the immediate post-war years, it is possible that this book might never have been written. Let me explain. After editing a club magazine for a while, imagine my surprise when I received a phone call from this legendary figure in Volkswagen circles. Boosted not

Right: A wacky occupation of students in the 1960s – cramming a car with as many bodies as possible in the often forlorn hope of breaking a world record while laudably raising money for charity. The fun Beetle was an ideal vehicle for such feats!

only by Ivan's kind words concerning my recent efforts but also by his warm invitation to meet with him to discuss his days at the Volkswagen plant, my 20-plus year passion for the marque escalated to 'must do more' fever pitch. A book about the Beetle had to be written, and now, some 18 titles later and a good number of years after Ivan Hirst's death, there is still a genuine delight in putting pen to paper about any subject involving those two great initials, V over W.

Similarly, I should thank the Bentley-owning schoolmaster who also drove a Beetle to work and who rejoiced in the name of 'Basher' Smith. It was he who made me think that if a Volkswagen could match such luxurious metal in deliberately reserved garage space, then such a car must be good enough for me too. Once bitten, of course, Volkswagens have been in the garage ever since!

Then there are the six Beetle owners whose magnificently original, or delightfully restored, cars form the highlights of the imagery in this book. Most, if not all, I have met at the various Volkswagen events held each summer for many a year. All have dedicated themselves in one way or another to the Volkswagen hobby, and each owns a car, or cars, that the Wolfsburg museum itself would be proud to display in their collection. To Phil Jarvis and his split-rear window Beetle, Phil Murgatroyd and his oval model, Robert Meekings and Simon Greaves joint owners of the later 1950s car, Vic Kaye and his 'one owner from new' Weltmeister, and Rob Loughrey with his multi prize-winning 1303 Cabriolet, I offer my heartfelt thanks.

Finally, I would like to thank another Volkswagen enthusiast of many years standing and my co-author on a relatively recent Transporter project. Knowledge of Brian Screaton's wonderfully extensive album of period press photographs and multi filing cabinet-filling anthology of sales brochures spurred me on to add more to my own collection and share some of them with everyone reading this book.

Richard A. Copping

Left: When the rich and famous adopted the Beetle, Volkswagen's advertising agency made sure they exploited the situation to the full. 'It's my car. I drive it every place I go' – Mr Paul Newman, Beverly Hills, California.

Left: Models or real cars? This image was used as the inside back cover illustration in the programme produced for the one-millionth Beetle celebrations.

1934–1945 PORSCHE'S NAZI BEETLE

Few consider it expedient to pronounce that without Hitler there would have been no Beetle. Many, including the archivists and historians at Volkswagen, choose to be selective in their recollections of the Beetle's origins, either over-emphasising Ferdinand Porsche's part in the process or simply blotting out the early years under the blanket heading of a government initiative. Most opt to paper neatly over the less savoury but unquestionably key aspects of the pre-1945 story.

The power behind dictatorship

In February 1933 at the annual Berlin Motor Show the newly elected Chancellor of Germany addressed the attendees. Neatly attired in a black jacket and pin-striped trousers and flanked by other members of his inner cabinet, the country's latest leader spoke authoritatively on matters close to the motor industry's heart. He foresaw a desperate need to reduce car taxes, relax Germany's oppressive traffic laws, and ease the road to the acquisition of a driving licence – three moves that would stimulate the path to car ownership in a country that lagged far behind many another in terms of motorisation. He spoke ambitiously of plans to build an unrivalled road system – the German autobahn network – and of the need for the German worker, who might currently rely on a motorcycle as his daily and even family transport, to be supplied with a small car at a realistic price.

Well received generally, even though amongst the more cynical members of Chancellor Hitler's audience there were those who believed this was a politician's way of securing additional votes in a forthcoming election, to one man the new leader's words were pure gold. He was the already renowned, superbly innovative but equally highly temperamental designer Ferdinand Porsche, creator of many of the German motor industry's most groundbreaking high-powered vehicles. However, Porsche's interests lay not just in the creation of the most expensive, the most highly-powered, the most luxurious machinery of his age, but also in a *Volkswagen* or *kleinauto*: a car for ordinary Germans to use as daily transport for work and at weekends for pleasure. When

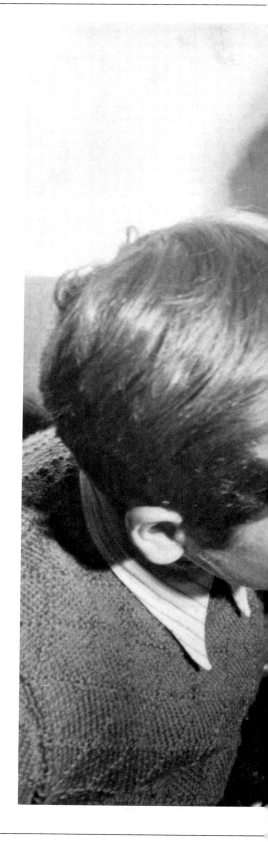

Right: Ferdinand Porsche pictured after the war when his part in the Beetle story was over. To the right is Ferdinand Piech, a future director general of Volkswagen AG.

Porsche heard Hitler speak he was no longer a young man with decades in front of him to pursue his goal; instead, a trail of failure in respect of aborted small car projects littered his wake. In the new Chancellor he probably saw his last chance.

Despite every aspect of the Hitler era of government being not only cast aside but also carefully obliterated from the German nation's records, the Nazi Party's creed castigated and its assets liquidated, the Third Reich's war not just lost but memory of its perpetrators partly expunged by suicide or execution, justifiably bitter recollections of the horrors of the time inevitably affected even the most fair-minded of historians who cast a shadow on each and every one of Hitler's motives both before and during his tenure of office. As a result, credence has been given to the theory that the autobahns were planned with thoughts of military movement in mind. Similarly, it has been argued that the dictator's determination with regard to the state's manufacture of a small car, even extending to the lengths of constructing a purpose-built factory for its mass production, was a clever ploy to guarantee facilities and technical knowhow for the construction of an invincible arsenal of vehicles with which Germany would crush all opposition in the pre-planned ensuing war.

However, surviving records analysed many years after the event suggest that on these occasions at least, Hitler's motives were genuine. Perhaps even the most malignant of dictators can produce a strategy of genuine benefit to those imprisoned under his bewitching control. The probability remains that Hitler's personal love of the automobile, his perception of its value to an entire nation and not just something restricted to the upper echelons of early 20th-century society – plus, coincidentally, his craving for the indulgence of powerfully fast Mercedes cars – arose from his reading of a biography of Henry Ford. Ford's undeniable anti-Semitism undoubtedly contributed to Hitler's empathy with this production genius, this builder of cars for the masses. Hitler chose to see in Ford's America unrivalled contentment, with motorisation available to all. If, with the implied wealth of Party leadership and, latterly, the attendant affluence of government, he could indulge in the purchase of the fastest and most luxurious of Mercedes saloons and convertibles, why shouldn't the *Volk* adulate him and worship the Party of which he was the leader as a result of the creation of an affordable German-built car designed specifically for them?

Having determined what was best for his people the dictator would countenance no opposition, and any such attempts from capitalist, self-indulgent German manufacturers would be dealt with accordingly. That such a philosophy suited an innocent if apparently politically naïve Ferdinand Porsche remains only too obvious, for the famous designer of numerous fast and expensive cars targeted at the rich, if not necessarily famous, had for many years been thwarted in his secret passion – the zeal to build a car for the people, a small car for those whose realistic ambition was to own a motorbike and probably nothing more.

Opposite top: Although identifiable as Beetles, the earliest prototypes – the VW3s – carried such features as suicide doors, headlamps on the front panel, and a short boot lid with knuckle-rasping handle, while they lacked a conventional rear window.

Opposite bottom: The second car of the series of three parked in Porsche's garden.

This page: This cluster of images all depict the first of the series of 30 prototypes known as the VW30. Between them the cars covered two million kilometres, making the Beetle the most exhaustively tested vehicle of all time. Although the VW30 still lacked a rear window there were many improvements over the specification of the VW3. The doors were larger, the headlamps had been relocated, and the lines of the revised body made the car appear more streamlined.

Porsche's passion to create a Volkswagen

From his first creation in 1900 (a one-off which his long-time private secretary Ghislaine Kaes described as a Voiturette) the designer persevered. Two decades later Porsche's third small car, a four-seat, all-aluminium-bodied vehicle named the Sascha, was designed during his time as general director of the Austro-Daimler Motor Company. With a four-cylinder inline water-cooled engine, a bore and stroke of 68mm and 75mm respectively, and a gross capacity of 1,100cc, this vehicle looked promising, but was cancelled at a point when no more than three prototypes had been built. The process of creating small but inherently efficient cars for the general public, rather than selling big cars to rich people, was of little interest to Austro-Daimler's board of directors.

Porsche was incensed by such an attitude, and when a somewhat complicated arrangement with the company's largest shareholder and bank was set to result in the dismissal of 2,000 employees he stormed out of a board meeting, his wishes foiled and his career at the company over.

At Daimler-Benz – Porsche's next employers, where he held the post of technical director – he once again pursued his goal of creating a small car, despite a feeling of indifference from his fellow directors. The vehicle that emerged was powered by a 25PS (*pferdestärken*, or metric horsepower) engine, with a bore and stroke of 68mm and 88mm and a compression ratio of 5.8:1. Maximum power was achieved at 3,300rpm. Promisingly, a total of 28 test vehicles were

built, some bodied as saloons and the rest as open tourers, but even then the project was not brought to fruition. Porsche's contract at Daimler-Benz was terminated amidst acrimonious recriminations regarding the design of the small car and his work with commercial vehicles.

Fortuitously for the feisty designer, work was readily available and in 1929 he joined the board of Vienna-based Steyrwerke, once more as technical director. While he was there his sixth small car took shape, but in only a matter of days after the 1929 Paris Auto Show Steyr's finances collapsed, and, to Porsche's immediate disadvantage, the company fell into the hands of the same bankers as those controlling Austro-Daimler. Although under the new management it was Porsche's latest large

Right: The VW30 on test on top of the world. Car 25 of the series is known to have covered in excess of 130,000km.

car project, rather than his work on a small vehicle, that was the initial victim of the axe, the decision to terminate a car that a short time ago had been the centre of attention at the Auto Show incensed him so much that he walked away from Steyr.

At the age of 55 and with no desire to be a dispensable cog in the wheel of a conglomerate any longer, Porsche decided to set up his own design studio, a move that came to fruition on 1 January 1931. His next small car project came about as the result of a commission offered by Fritz Neumeyer of the motorcycle manufacturer Zündapp Gmbh. Like Porsche he was convinced of the need for, and the viability of, producing a *kleinauto*. The vehicle that began to take shape was the first to carry both a visual and mechanical resemblance to the Beetle of a few years hence. Admittedly, the rear-

mounted radial engine was of the water-cooled variety, but only because Neumeyer insisted that air-cooled engines were too noisy. Porsche's then recently patented and revolutionary torsion bars were present as might be expected, as was the far from universally accepted notion of a rear-mounted power plant. For the designer, the project looked more promising than anything had for some considerable time. However, as 1932 began to unfurl it became increasingly obvious that the project would run out of steam. Prototype testing had borne witness to engines that boiled over with monotonous regularity and torsion bars that shattered with irritating predictability. The axe hovered over the project until it finally fell when Neumeyer came to realise just how costly the essential stamping presses required to form the final steel body parts would be.

Disillusioned, he cancelled the project; a despondent Porsche was paid off, his dream shattered yet again.

However, all was not lost, as during 1933 Porsche was given the opportunity to take the small car project one stage further as the result of an approach by Fritz von Falkenhayn, the head of NSU. Rumour has it that modifications to the design for the Zündapp vehicle had already been made both at Porsche's personal expense and in his own time; certainly the prototypes produced for NSU appeared with amazing alacrity and carried all the advances required from the previous project but few if any of its faults. As before, torsion bars were an intrinsic part of the vehicle's make-up, while parallel trailing arms were employed at the front and swing axles at the rear. Free from the constraints set by Zündapp, the engine, although still

Below: Three Beetles were present at the factory foundation-stone laying ceremony held on 26 May 1938. These cars, often known as the VW303 series, were important as not only were they the first to feature the characteristic split rear window, but they also clearly illustrated the intention to build three variations on the Beetle theme: a straightforward saloon, a sunroof model, and a cabriolet.

mounted at the car's rear, was an air-cooled flat-four. Offering a maximum of 26PS, the 1,470cc unit had one unusual characteristic for the time, a feature that would become one of the key properties of the Beetle, namely its maximum speed being achieved at just 2,600rpm.

Once again, however, fate was to conspire to deprive Porsche of his goal.

Firstly, von Falkenhayn had growing concerns about raising the necessary investment required to build the small car. Secondly, NSU's motorcycle sales were sufficiently buoyant that it seemed unlikely the company had the desired capacity to meet the demand, let alone to take on an additional project. Thirdly, and crucially, Italian manufacturers

Fiat, who had become aware of the project, reminded the German firm of an agreement signed between the two whereby NSU would never build a four-wheeled vehicle under its own name. Porsche's creation was in direct contravention of this; he must have thought that the end of his personal crusade had been reached.

A meeting of the like-minded

As has already been established, not only was Porsche present when Hitler made his speech at the Berlin Motor Show in 1933, but he also liked what he heard so much that – to the exclusion of all other considerations – he scurried away to start work on a paper he was determined to present to the Reich Ministry of Transport, outlining his design ideas for the construction of a *kleinauto*, a small car for the German people. On this occasion, at long last, rather than being thwarted by either benign or malevolent interests, destiny played into his hands.

Porsche was both acquainted with, and sympathetic to, one Jakob Werlin. Their relationship, if it could be called that, had arisen during Porsche's period in the employ of Daimler-Benz, where Werlin, then the company's representative in Munich, had defended his designs and ideas in some of the heated boardroom battles. The salesman had risen to albeit unofficial prominence by maintaining an influential and advisory relationship with Hitler after selling the Nazi Party leader his first Mercedes years before, in 1923.

Now, at the most appropriate of moments, Werlin appeared at Porsche's studio, only to hurry back to Hitler to report the designer's ambitions. Hitler having already met and been impressed by Porsche in the context of an Auto Union Racing Project, now wished to see him once more.

Recent but not totally proven research suggests that Hitler and Porsche met at the Hotel Kaiserhof in late August or early September 1933. (Others suggest the meeting took place after Porsche had delivered his design and construction thoughts on the subject of a small car in January 1934, but if this really was the case, why, when the contents of Porsche's subsequent report are assessed, was such a repetitious assembly necessary?) Hitler apparently spoke at length and with knowledgeable detail about the car he wanted: a vehicle suitable for a family with up to three children, something that would be economical to run and yet was much more than a three-wheeler. For once wily, Porsche took careful note of the dictator's apparent preference for an engine mounted at the front of the car

in the traditional manner, and his less conventional desires for both air-cooling of the block and the use of diesel to fuel the vehicle; after all, each of these was recommended in the latest car magazines that any enthusiast, including Hitler, would be likely to read. What Porsche found extremely difficult to countenance was Hitler's insistence that the selling price of such a small car would be set below 1,000 Marks, when both the Zündapp and NSU vehicles would have retailed at a price at least double that, if not more.

Once a buoyant Hitler had left the meeting, Werlin suggested that Porsche should prepare exactly what he was already in the process of working on, and compile his thoughts on the subject of a small car in the form of a report for the Führer. One copy would inevitably go direct to the dictator, the door having been left suitably ajar; another should be presented through the official channels of the Ministry of Transport; and, of course, another had to be delivered to the cunning, opportunistic Jakob Werlin.

Blueprint for the Beetle

Porsche's Exposé was duly delivered on 17 January 1934 and proved to be the necessary blueprint required to develop the Beetle. In recognition of what Hitler had requested Porsche defined the *Volksauto* in five crucial statements of what the car should and should not be:

1 A volkswagen should not be a small car whose dimensions are reduced at the expense of both handling and life

expectancy, while it remains relatively heavy. Instead, it should be a functional car of standard dimensions but comparatively low weight, an objective that can be achieved by fundamentally new processes.

2 A volkswagen should not be a small car with limited power at the expense of maximum speed and good climbing ability, but rather a practical vehicle with the necessary power to achieve

normal maximum speeds and climbing abilities.

3 A volkswagen should not be a small car with reduced passenger space at the expense of comfort, but instead it should be a fully functional vehicle with normal – or, rather, comfortable – space within the bodywork.

4 A volkswagen should not be a vehicle with limited uses, but instead should be capable of fulfilling all conceivable

purposes by simply exchanging the bodywork, for use not only as a passenger car but also as a commercial vehicle and for certain military purposes.

5 A volkswagen should not be fitted with unnecessarily complicated equipment requiring increased servicing, but should rather be a vehicle with, as far as possible, simple and foolproof equipment, reducing servicing to an absolute minimum.

To achieve all the requirements of the nation's volkswagen, Porsche specified: the best possible suspension and handling; a maximum speed in the region of 100kph; a climbing ability of around 30 per cent; a closed full four-seat body for the passengers; the lowest possible purchase price; and, finally, the most economical of running costs. As a result of this specification the design demanded:

a wheelbase of 2,500mm and a track of 1,200mm to accommodate a potential five occupants; an engine offering a maximum of 26PS at a lowly 3,500rpm, to ensure sufficient power and the required longevity; a kerb weight of 650kg, making sure an average fuel consumption of eight litres per 100km was possible for economy; and a full swing axle. Daringly, Porsche suggested that the selling price of such a vehicle would be an affordable 1,550 Reichmarks.

Shortly after presenting his Exposé Porsche was informed that the RDA (the Reich Association of the German Automobile Industry) would be working with him to produce a volkswagen. However reluctant the trade association of German car manufacturers might have been, the organisation was only too aware that the Führer's wishes were also now his commands.

The Führer wishes

Hitler's speech at the Berlin Motor Show of March 1934 was anything but conciliatory to the motor trade or anyone else he thought might stall or delay his will. During the brief period of 12 months since the previous show the atmosphere had changed completely. Hitler wore full uniform, while the show's halls were bedecked with the regalia of Nazi domination. The Führer's will had become absolute.

'Germany has only one automobile for every 100 of its people. France on the other hand has one for each 28, while the USA has one for every six of its citizens. That disparity will be changed. I wish to see a mass-produced German-built car that can be bought by anyone who has the income to afford a motorbike. Simple, reliable, economical transport is required. We must have a real car for the German people – a *volkswagen*.'

Left: The propaganda value of being seen travelling in the KdF-Wagen was invaluable to Hitler.

Evolution to presentable prototype

Porsche's contract to build Germany's small car was issued on 22 June 1934. The timescale was tight, but not totally unachievable. Porsche was given six months to design the vehicle and an additional four months to build just one prototype. However, there was a major stumbling block, one that would define the Beetle as it is known today: that issue, so clearly defined in the contract, remained – as might have been anticipated – one of cost and affordability. The design had to evolve around a selling price of 900 Reichmarks, a figure which was to be calculated on mass production of 50,000 units and the gross material costs per vehicle therein; the wages that would have to be paid for producing each car; and the application of the industry standard of a 200 per cent surcharge on those wages. Porsche had little option but to reduce the weight of both the body and chassis when compared to those of his more recent prototypes for other projects. Similarly, although a whole spectrum of

prototype engines were progressed over a relatively lengthy period, the final design choice, and coincidentally Hitler's original preference, was selected on the triple criteria of reliability, weight or the lack of it, and, most important of all, cost.

As the Porsche design office lacked attendant workshop facilities use was made of the conveniently spacious garage attached to the family home, which was also the recipient of essential equipment in the car assembly business and included a milling machine, two lathes, and a drill press. The prototypes were constructed from purpose-built components made by firms contracted specifically for the volkswagen project. The monthly fees paid to Porsche were initially set at 20,000 Reichmarks per month, but subsequently increased to first 30,000 and then 40,000, before a relatively short period of intense activity when the figure rose to 50,000 Reichmarks. Likewise, by 1935 Porsche's staff had increased to a total of 33 engineers, supplemented by a workshop

crew of five, the latter being augmented by a further seven men during 1936.

By the onset of winter in 1935 the Porsche team had built two cars, having been granted the authority to build three prototypes instead of the original one as early as 7 December 1934, the V1 being a saloon and the V2 a cabriolet. By February 1936 the first of a trio of V3 prototypes was ready, in July Hitler was shown two of the series, and on 12 October five vehicles, including the two original test cars, were presented to the RDA ready for assessment, as stipulated in the now considerably elongated contract. The V3 series had been built with the assistance of Daimler-Benz and included such prototype peculiarities as wooden-framed bodies, although one vehicle at least was of all-steel construction. All, even the earliest examples, had been upgraded to include the latest engine.

In appearance these very early prototypes bore more than a passing resemblance to the finished product of a few years later. The wheelbase stood at 2,400mm, the track at 1,250mm at both front and rear, independent suspension was provided in the form of torsion bars, the engine was installed behind the rear axle, the gearbox forward of it, while the tyres varied between 4.50 x 17 and 4.50 x 16. The familiar Beetle shape, with its streamlined shell fitted to a tubular platform frame, had emerged, but the cars lacked a recognisable rear window, its place being taken by a large engine lid complete with prominent louvres cut into it in its upper regions. They also lacked running boards, featured rear-hinged (or suicide) doors, and the boot lid was cut short to allow the vehicle's headlamps to be placed on this central section of the car's front, a move which resulted in many a scraped knuckle when attempting to open the lid.

Porsche's team had worked hard to stay within the weight limits set out in the Exposé, nevertheless gradually edged towards 416.76kg for the chassis (which appears to have been more or less completed by the end of the first quarter

Below: From the very early days it was planned that a sunroof model should be an integral part of the range. This image was included in the pre-war brochure to promote the KdF-Wagen.

Left: Bearing the chassis number 31, the car depicted is the 1938 Cabriolet now resident in Wolfsburg's Stiftung Museum.

Below: The KdF-Wagen factory under construction.

of 1935) and 246kg for the bodywork, which was still at the study stage by the middle of 1935. Fortunately, both figures allowed scope for any further necessary development without endangering the guiding principles.

The question of an engine suitable to power the Beetle was one that was going to tax the Porsche team's skills more than most. That the unit powering the V3 series when it was presented for testing had the designation 'E-motor' serves to demonstrate how many attempts had preceded it, each of which had been aborted at some stage of its progress. To comply with the self-imposed demands he had set himself in the Exposé, Porsche's first preference was to develop a simple two-stroke engine, by design lightweight in nature – a factor guaranteed through the use of magnesium or aluminium to a greater or lesser part in its construction – with a projected but realistic output of 26PS achieved at a leisurely maximum of 3,200rpm, an assumed capacity of one litre, and an ability to run on a 40:1 mixture of petrol and oil.

Above: The VW38 prototypes were paraded around Germany in a well-planned campaign to increase interest in the KdF-Wagen to fever pitch, while journalists were invited to test-drive the car and promote its capabilities.

Bernard Wiersch, one-time archivist and chief historian at Volkswagen, relayed the words of Josef Kales, a colleague of Porsche's, to confirm the diversity of units that were attempted to comply with the professor's wishes: 'A range of air-cooled two-stroke engines were built: twin-cylinder, three-cylinder, double piston units with larger inlet piston than exhaust piston, others with pistons of similar sizes, some with scavenging pumps, some mounted longitudinally in the tail or

transversely in unit with the transmission, and so on.'

Sadly for those involved, all the two-stroke engines – including a toyed-with Type A5 with different bore diameters and a cubic capacity of 960cc, and the Type 60D with overhead camshaft and a capacity of 800cc – proved persistently problematical when tested, as none was ever really gas-tight, and for this reason if no other they were eventually dropped from the programme in favour of another contender capable of

fulfilling the criteria within budget. This took the form of an air-cooled four-cylinder boxer four-stroke engine, which Porsche thought should have a capacity of 1.25 litres, from which 26PS could be developed at a maximum of 3,500rpm. Later Porsche was to confirm that although the cost of such a unit would be a little higher than a twin-cylinder engine, it had decided benefits; advantages which came in the shape of a greater degree of elasticity, comparatively subdued engine noise levels, and, for the future, greater

compatibility with the demands of any likely export market.

The specification of the four-cylinder boxer unit that emerged and was destined to prove reliable in forthcoming tests varied slightly from Porsche's intentions in that its cubic capacity stood at 900, while output was calculated to be 22PS achieved at a maximum of 3,100rpm. The bore stood at 70mm and the stroke at 64mm. The four-speed gearbox facilitated a maximum speed of 100kph.

From 10 October to 22 December 1936 three V3s took part in what was then an unparalleled series of long-distance test runs, the results of which were to lead to the creation of the next set of prototypes. Drivers from Porsche's staff, with accompanying observers supplied by the RDA, criss-crossed the country on all types of roads. Although the grand total of some 31,000 miles revealed that there were some problems to iron out, the report produced by the RDA was positive, despite

that body's self-interest in seeing the Beetle at least delayed and at best abandoned: 'A number of shortfalls in the car were discovered in the 50,000 kilometres covered in the tests. However, they aren't of a fundamental nature and it is expected that they can be overcome technically without a great deal of difficulty. Both performance and handling characteristics are good; the vehicle has shown qualities which would appear to recommend further development.'

Above: This VW38 has survived and is resident at Wolfsburg.

The W30

The revisions deemed necessary were executed with considerable speed and the revised Beetle design was presented to the Daimler-Benz body plant at Sindelfingen, where, as the project number might imply, 30 cars were built. All had steel bodies, 29 of the run being saloons and the one remaining vehicle a demonstrator cabriolet. For their work Daimler-Benz were paid 140,918 Reichmarks. Although the look of the Beetle had evolved with, for example, the headlights becoming an integral part of the front wings, many characteristics of the final car were still absent. Suicide doors were still part of the Volkswagen's make-up, although

these were now larger, so that the rear side-windows had to be unusually small and would have resulted in an even more claustrophobic feel for rear-seat passengers. The lack of a proper rear window and the knuckle-scraping boot lid were also still evident. Eventually some of the series were fitted with bumpers, while the cabriolet – which was little more than the V2 with a new steel chassis and a rebuilt front end – also benefited from running boards.

Possibly most interesting was that the air-cooled boxer engine had been refined, resulting in a power output of 24.8PS achieved at a maximum of 3,000rpm. The compression ratio was 5.8:1, although the recorded maximum speed remained constant at 100kph.

If trials of the V3 series cars had been unprecedented in their extent, they were as nothing when compared to those of the W30. On this occasion 120 specially selected members of the SS were seconded for the job. The cars were parked at the tank barracks of Kornwestheim near Stuttgart, where there was ample space for

servicing – an essential requirement when long-distance testing was planned. The 30 vehicles, which were all thoroughly run-in before the tests started, covered a grand total of close on 1.95 million kilometres. Inevitably individual mileages varied greatly; some cars were written off, the demonstration cabriolet covered no more than 12,000km, a typical low-mileage vehicle might have covered roughly double that figure, while some successfully accomplished in excess of 150,000km.

With the cost of building the cars already revealed, the trials brought the total up to a staggering 1.7 million Reichmarks. However, every trip had been recorded in great detail. While the overall results, which were still in the process of compilation as late as mid-1938, confirmed that Porsche's design was not only eminently practical but also way ahead of its time, they also served to illustrate that some work had been required during the test process and that further refinements must be contemplated before series production could be guaranteed.

The VW38 – the Beetle comes of age

Although most gloss over the intricacies of prototype designations, by the time the Beetle had taken the recognisable form in which it continued to be produced in post-war Germany, and was lined up to receive the adulation of the crowd at the factory's foundation-stone laying ceremony, it was known by three specific designations that more or less refer to the same style of vehicle. First came three hurriedly prepared vehicles: a saloon, a sunroof model, and a cabriolet, which were branded as V303s. These were the cars that were required to be present at the aforementioned ceremony. Then came the VW38 series, named not for the total number produced, but from the year in which they were constructed; these were the vehicles which were used to promote the 'Strength through Joy' (*Kraft durch Freude*) cars to the masses. Publicity tours started in the autumn of 1938 and continued well into the summer

of 1939, when the VW38 series had been joined by newer brethren, which, apart from showing signs of minor and usually technical revisions, bore the designation VW39.

Although different in technical specification detail – for example, the track of the VW38 series had altered from a standard 1,250mm both front and rear with the VW30, to 1,290mm and 1,250mm respectively, while the weight of the latest prototype series stood at a comparatively hefty 750kg at least compared to the featherweight 650kg of its predecessor – it was in its appearance that the VW38 had changed most. The Porsche team had gleaned sufficient information from the performance of the previous prototypes, and a great deal more from detailed wind tunnel research, to recognise that the shape of the Beetle could be improved considerably. Ferdinand Porsche duly commissioned the Stuttgart-

This page: The Schwimmwagen was undoubtedly the most ingenious of Porsche's military vehicles based on the Beetle. Two versions existed: the first, designated the Type 128, was the larger, while the second, the Type 166, was produced in far greater numbers.

Opposite: The body of what appears to be a regular KdF-Wagen being lowered on to its chassis during the war years. The eagle-eyed might be able to spot a near-complete Kübelwagen in the background.

based coachwork company of Wilhelm Reutter to build the VW38 series, starting with a wooden mock-up of what had been planned. This was then viewed by most of the Porsche design team, who requested just two further refinements – complete integration of the headlamps into the front wings in the graceful style that would be a hallmark of the Beetle for the best part of the next 30 years, and a modification to the style of the rear lights, which was of far less significance. Porsche employee Erwin Komenda's soon to be famous split rear window made its debut, as did the universal incorporation of both running boards and bumpers. Key to the advance was the streamlining of the all-steel bodywork, while the potentially dangerous rear-hinged doors were banished in favour

of model front-hinged affairs. The Beetle was indeed born!

Before war broke out attendees at either the factory foundation-stone laying ceremony or the 1939 Berlin Motor Show, held in early March, seemed to treat the Beetle with a surprising level of indifference. The writer of an article in *Practical Motorist*, for example, summarised the Beetle as 'a practical little machine, which should achieve the purpose with which it was conceived, namely, to bring motoring within the reach of all classes of the German people. Its design is certainly advanced, but there is nothing extraordinary about it, nor anything a British manufacturer might not equal if he had the same advantages (or disadvantages) of state control.' Little did they realise!

The creation of a Nazi-owned manufacturing company

Separate to Porsche's development of the Volkswagen and not necessarily in chronological sequence with its progression, although equally vital to its long-term survival, was a decision born as a result of deliberate but ill-advised procrastination by members of the RDA. Hitler's mounting anger, so clearly demonstrated in the speech he spat out at the Berlin Motor Show in 1937, covered the lamentable lack of progress and his recognition of the ongoing and seemingly countenanced hesitancy with which those charged with creating the Volkswagen believed they could stall production of the state car indefinitely:

'It is my irrevocable decision to make the German automobile industry, one of our greatest industries, independent from the insecurities of imports and by so doing place it on a solid, secure base. Let there be no doubt – so-called private business is either capable of dealing with this issue or it is not competent to continue as private business. The National Socialist State will under no circumstances capitulate to the convenience, the limitations, or the ill-will of individual Germans.'

As a clear demonstration of his threat that no other *kleinauto* would be permitted, Hitler stormed away from the Opel stand where the ageing and apparently

politically unaware Herr von Opel had appeared delighted to show the Führer the company's new P4, a small car marketed as 'the car of the little man'. Shortly after this incident Opel and other manufacturers found it increasingly difficult to obtain the materials necessary to build such cars, while when word circulated that the company planned to reduce the price of the P4 by 200 Reichmarks to an even more affordable 1,250 RM, allegedly unofficial but still sufficiently menacing messages were sent to the effect that price cuts of this nature would not be tolerated.

To suggest that the RDA's proposal that each German manufacturer could either supply a number of parts for Porsche's *kleinauto*, or build a set number of Volkswagens alongside their normal production lines, was not well received would be an understatement; and the alternative proposal that a manufacturer would be willing to turn over the greater part of his assembly line to building the state's small car providing a 200RM subsidy was forthcoming was met with undisguised hostility.

Speaking on 26 May 1938, henchman and head of the German Labour Front Robert Ley declared that it was 'the Führer's will that within a few years no less than six million volkswagens would be on Germany's roads.' To achieve this,

Above: In the region of 1,500 cars with KdF-Wagen bodywork were built during the war years. The majority were Type 82E models, a military version with spartan appointments but with the advantage of the Kübel's chassis and consequent greater ground clearance of 290mm. The picture shows a Type 82E being filled up with wood chips for its gas generator.

production would start at 150,000 cars a year but rapidly escalate to 1.5 million vehicles annually. 'In ten years time,' declared Ley, 'nobody in Germany who is capable of working will not own a Volkswagen.' To secure the accomplishment of such lofty intentions Hitler and the Nazi Party would ride roughshod over the RDA, removing any vestige of influence it had once enjoyed as a penalty for its ill-considered stalling. The solution was simple: with the financial security of the nation's wealth available there was nothing to prevent the Nazis from founding a company for the specific purpose of manufacturing the Volkswagen and building a factory dedicated to that role.

The Volkswagen Development Company, or *Gesellschaft zur Vorbereitung des Volkswagens* (in turn abbreviated to *Gezuvor*, or 'After you'), was formed in late May 1937 with capital of 480,000 Reichmarks at its disposal. The board of management consisted of Ferdinand Porsche, Jakob Werlin, and Bodo Lafferentz, assistant to Ley, the man whose organisation was the provider of both the initial and later even more substantial funding. Porsche now had all the financial resources he required at his fingertips: Nazi money, government money, the two were as one in the unholy alliance that formed the backbone of the Third Reich, and this would prove to be a crucial point in the Beetle's story of survival against the odds when the question of ownership arose in post-war Germany.

A home for the Beetle

The location and the scale of the factory created by the Nazis, indeed its very existence, would prove to be of great significance in the story of the Beetle's post-war survival. Hitler had asserted that the purpose-built Beetle plant should be erected in central Germany and that access by all means of transport must be excellent. Bodo Lafferentz settled on land north of the Mittelland Canal on the Lüneberg Heath, close to the village of Fallersleben and encompassing much of the estates of two families: the von der Schulenburgs, who resided in Wolfsburg Castle, yielded 7,600 acres, the von der Wenses were to forego 2,500 acres, while 28 smaller landowners were deprived of the remaining 4,900 acres that made up the factory and attendant site on both sides of the canal. Although apparently remote, the Mittelland Canal linked the location with the ports of Bremen in the west and Hamburg in the north, while to the east it connected with Berlin, Prague, and even the River Oder. Furthermore, rail connections were close by and Hitler's network of autobahns was well on its way to completion, making road connections equally good. The location was consequently ideal, and its comparative seclusion and virgin freshness meant that it wasn't even

marked on many maps – which, bearing in mind what the not too distant future held in store, was a distinct advantage when it came to avoiding war damage.

As the factory was a state or Nazi Party project through and through its scale was inevitably vast, as befitted any monument to the cult of the Führer. In its plan it emulated the mass-production showpiece Ford plant at River Rouge, but even this was to be dwarfed, as the factory front was designed to stretch to 1,350m, or three-quarters of a mile. By the outbreak of war in September 1939 four massive halls and the all-important power station had been built, more than sufficient for production to begin at the rate planned by Porsche and the Nazis. Hall One took the form of a tool and dye shop covering 420,000sq ft and of a scale sufficient to cope with planned future expansion of up to one million cars annually; Hall Two was a press shop of 447,000sq ft; Hall Three at 775,000sq ft was the largest and was devoted to a combination of paint shop, body framing, and final assembly; while Hall Four, the second largest at 527,000sq ft, was committed to the machining of parts and the completion of mechanical sub-assemblies. Any presence on this kind of scale was likely to prove difficult to eradicate.

Compulsory purchase

Hitler's demand of his lieutenants that Germany should be motorised within a matter of a few short years required considerable resourcefulness on their part if there was to be any chance of fulfilling his wishes. His much-vaunted order that the car Porsche was working on should not cost more than 1,000 Reichmarks was, apart from playing a crucial part in the successful specification we know today, one of practical politics. Many citizens of the Reich, and particularly those most attracted to the Nazi cause, earned from as little as 160 to no more than 500 Reichmarks per month. Hard times had also resulted in the savings of many having dropped below 1,000 Reichmarks by the time Hitler came to power. A device had to be employed to encourage, possibly even force, the German nation to buy the Beetle and it came in the form of an instalment plan devised by and administered under the auspices of the German Labour Front, the DAF (*Die Deutsche Arbeitsfront*), and its subsidiary recreation and leisure-time body, the Strength through Joy movement or KdF (*Kraft durch Freude*), which in turn sponsored the car out of its annual income of some 80 million Reichmarks per year.

DAF boss Robert Ley launched the scheme on 1 August 1938, denouncing exclusivity and proclaiming that every German citizen, regardless of class, status, or material possessions, could register to buy a Volkswagen. All that was required was that a minimum of five Reichmarks, inclusive of insurance, should be saved every week. The hard-sell of the scheme that followed allowed those earning above 200 to 300 Reichmarks per month to take out an individual subscription, while lower earners were persuaded to club together in what amounted to a group subscription; it even gave the opportunity for those with more money in their pockets to 'invest' larger sums per week should they so desire.

Although there is no evidence that the scheme wasn't a genuine one, despite post-war claims that the Nazi regime wanted the cash amassed for military purposes, neither was it a particularly favourable arrangement for any but the State. While opening a layaway account was considered to be equivalent to ordering a car, there was no guarantee given regarding the final price of the vehicle, or even that a Volkswagen would be available when the final instalment had been made. Furthermore, anyone who missed a mandatory payment, or who decided that it was no longer possible to allocate such a sum each week, was threatened with the distinct possibility of losing everything they had put into the scheme.

Nevertheless, just short of 270,000 people signed up virtually immediately, a number equal to more than twice the General Motors-owned Opel's annual production. By the time war came in the early autumn of 1939, 336,668 German *Volk* had contributed a massive 280 million Reichmarks. If the unthinkable had happened, and Hitler and the Nazis had won the war, it is just conceivable that the Beetle would have still become the phenomenon it was later to prove, but under a very different set of circumstances.

War eclipses the Beetle's projected star

Hitler's declaration of war very nearly resulted in the Beetle becoming nothing more than a series of prototypes that had been extensively tested and then discarded. Hitler's and the Nazi hierarchy's grandiose claims suggesting such glaringly ludicrous production figures as 100,000 cars for 1940 – a total which rapidly grew to an astonishing 450,000 within months of the original announcement – more or less immediately withered away to nothing. The KdF factory might well have appeared to an outsider as a costly white elephant, particularly as there appeared at first to be no great rush to turn the buildings over to the manufacture of military vehicles.

It would be 1941 before the first cars were built at the KdF factory rather than elsewhere, and even then they totalled no more than 41 vehicles, produced at the staggering cost of 8,000 Reichmarks each. The following year saw 157 Beetles emerge, each priced to sell at 4,614RM. In total, before a fourth and final bombing raid on

Below: A four-wheel-drive version of the Type 82E, given the designation Type 87 and known as the Kommandeurwagen, was built in small numbers, the majority of which were destined for Rommel's Afrika Korps.

the factory occurred in the high summer of 1944, 630 cars that could not be mistaken for military vehicles had been built, with a passing resemblance to the Volkswagen. Without exception these cars were set aside for use by anyone other than the people the Beetle had been designed for. Some were channelled towards Nazi Party dignitaries for their personal wartime use, Robert Ley being a case in point. Others were gifted to friends of the Party such as Jakob Werlin, or were required by the Porsche office for further development purposes, while political diplomacy demanded that some were presented to, for example, Germany's ally the Japanese Emperor Hirohito and Herr Messerschmitt, the latter in a scurrilously blatant attempt to remind the beneficiary of the KdF factory's potential to manufacture items divorced from car production.

Military incarnations of the Beetle

Below: The Kübel-sitz-Wagen, shortened to Kübelwagen or 'bucket car,' designed to be an all-terrain vehicle, evolved from a modified KdF-Wagen into the Type 82. The vehicle pictured dates from the latter years of the war, a time when fuel shortages were acute. A number of Kübelwagens were adapted to burn wood gas – carbon monoxide.

Of Ferdinand Porsche's and the KdF factory's wartime activities away from the Beetle, one creation is of more interest than all the others put together. The vehicle in question was Germany's all-terrain equivalent of the American Jeep, the *Kübelwagen*. Inevitably variations on the theme emerged, but the genre is epitomised by the two-wheel drive model known as the Type 82, which is generally recognised to have been past the prototype stage by the latter months of 1939, before entering somewhat spasmodic production in the early months of the following year. Certainly records indicate that by 20 December 1940 1,000 such vehicles had been built. More recent research, however, casts doubt on the long promulgated theory that it was only in 1943 that the vehicle received an upgraded engine as per the military's well-known stipulation that all vehicles in their 'employ' must have at least 25PS at their disposal.

The requested more powerful engine appeared during the course of 1943; exactly when appears to be a matter of controversy, although, other than to confirm that this option became the property of all Beetle saloons produced from this point onwards to the total exclusion of the original unit, the debate is somewhat irrelevant. Cubic capacity was increased from the original 985 to 1,131cc. Bore was expanded from 70 to 75mm, but the stroke remained at 64mm, while the compression ratio now stood at 5.8:1. Although *pferdestärken* only increased from 23.5 to 25PS (a maximum that was achieved at 3,200rpm rather than 3,000), augmented torque proved particularly useful when heavier bodies were placed on what had been intended to be nothing more than a chassis for the people's car.

Assessing a saloon assembled in the early days of British control at the former KdF factory, Humber reported thus on the bigger engine, albeit somewhat inaccurately in terms of the exact specification of what was being examined: 'We understand that the engine capacity has been increased from 960cc's [sic] of ... earlier model[s] to 1161cc's for this civilian saloon model. The engine is of course of the horizontally opposed 4-cylinder air-cooled type, employing push rod operated overhead valves with a forced draught air cooling employing a blower mounted on the top of the engine.'

In line with the general sentiments expressed concerning the Beetle, Humber clearly thought the engine posed little or no threat to the British automobile industry and the power units they had developed earlier. Today, and possibly with the benefit of hindsight, this level of complacency implies a degree of naivety in relation to Porsche's product, or possibly an assessment clouded by the wartime propaganda opinion that all things German were bad.

'The engine is somewhat noisy and rough', the Humber report continues, 'and no doubt the absence of water jacketing and soft mounting are responsible for this. As will be seen from the performance and petrol consumption figures ... the performance is by no means outstanding but the consumption figure is quite good, although of course this is partly due to the extreme lightness of the vehicle. The

size of the carburettor and induction pipe suggests that more power could be obtained from the engine as these parts appear to have been deliberately reduced in size, but whether the engine is capable of withstanding an increased power output is a debatable point.'

Two further military vehicles are worthy of mention: one for its unusual abilities which have ensured it retains both a curiosity interest and an enthusiast following, and the other due to its likeness in appearance to the Beetle saloon.

The appropriately named *Schwimmwagen* was born out of the success in military service of the Kübelwagen. Germany had amphibious vehicles at its disposal to further the war effort, but it was considered by the Army Office of armaments that a Porsche-led creation would perform better. The result was a Kübelwagen-type body with a watertight tub-style base welded from sheet steel, backed by sufficient rubber seals to prevent leaks where the shell had to be penetrated to accommodate items like the steering arms and drive shafts. Unlike the Kübelwagen, the amphibious Schwimmwagen was designed to operate with or without four-wheel drive and benefited from an additional gear calculated to assist on cross-country expeditions. The extra gear was engaged via a dual-purpose lever, its other role being to either select or take the vehicle out of four-wheel-drive mode. The engine was concealed in a waterproof compartment at the rear. When used in water, although the wheels kept turning – and in the case of the front ones continued to steer the car – vehicle movement was provided by a three-blade propeller.

In 1941 a second version of the Schwimmwagen was commissioned, this time by the High Command of the SS, who had been suitably impressed by the original model. The original amphibious vehicle had been allocated the type number 128; the later Schwimmwagen, an altogether more compact affair, became the Type 166. The wheelbase was reduced by 400mm compared to that of the Type 128, the width of the vehicle was reduced by 100mm, and the overall weight was 10kg lighter, despite the provision of a second fuel tank that increased the vehicle's range by some 80km. The Type 166 carried both the running gear and transmission of the earlier model and also benefited from reduction gearing fitted to the half-axles, the additional low cross-country gear and four-wheel drive when required, and, inevitably, a watertight compartment for the engine.

In addition to the few Volkswagens built during the war years, vehicles that looked like the Beetle but bore characteristics of military incarnations on the Volkswagen theme also emerged. The Type 82E was essentially a KdF saloon with particularly spartan appointments, as suited a military vehicle, mated to the Kübelwagen's chassis. This gave the vehicle increased ground clearance of 290mm, making it much more versatile for use on a variety of terrains. When supplied to the SS such vehicles were given the designation 92SS, but displayed no characteristics different to the 82E, which in turn was powered, as were all military manifestations, by the standard Beetle engine of the day.

More unusual and certainly only built in small numbers was the vehicle that was given the semi-official title of the *Kommandeurwagen* and the type number VW87. Issued primarily to commanders operating in Rommel's Afrika Korps, the VW87 was designed to be driven where roads or even tracks didn't exist. With the body of a Beetle, as per the Type 82E, and with a similar trim level, the Kommandeurwagen was mechanically more or less identical to the two designs of Schwimmwagen. Four-wheel drive could be selected as and when required, although normally the rear wheels would do the work. The extra low cross-country gear was part of its specification, while the vehicle also stood higher off the ground, like other members of the military ensemble. Bearing in mind their planned destination, most Kommandeurwagens were fitted with the folding fabric sunroof originally proposed as an option or sub-model within the KdF saloon range. Extra equipment in the form of ducting to protect the engine, and especially the electrics, was standard for vehicles destined for North Africa, while some cars were fitted with massive sand tyres, necessitating modification of the front axle.

A car with an uncertain future?

Hitler's defeat should have spelt extermination for his car, a product of Nazi money, a vehicle even bearing an absurd Nazi name – not that many outside the nucleus of the Reich paid more than lip service to such blatant propaganda.

Known variously as the Volksauto or most commonly the Volkswagen – the term *Volk* having a nationalistic significance in Germany greater than the literal translation of 'folk' or 'people' – most of those present at the factory foundation-stone laying ceremony of 26 May 1938 had been somewhat surprised, or even dismayed, that Hitler decreed that the latter-stage Beetle prototypes before them would be given the lacklustre and internationally less than palatable name of the *KdF-Wagen*, or 'Strength through Joy' car.

Curiously the main demand made in Hitler's speech that day would be achieved, although not in the manner he envisaged: 'When I came to power in 1933, I recognised one problem that had to be dealt with at once; the issue of motorising the nation. … The first step towards putting an end to [Germany being behind everyone else] was to get rid of the idea that a motorcar is a luxury. What I wish is not a car for 200,000 or 300,000 people who have the money to afford it, but an automobile which six million or seven million can afford.'

Few, if any, would have thought in May 1945 that there would be any more Beetles at all, but in time the war years would come to be regarded as simply a period of stagnation in the Beetle's history, a potentially costly delay in the launch of a design that by 1945 was already approaching the tenth anniversary of its conception. Fortunately for the Beetle, a general consequence of war was that other manufacturers' design aspirations likewise ground to a halt, ensuring that if antiquity could be an issue in any planned revival of the Volkswagen's fortunes, rivals were similarly affected.

1945–1949 BRITISH BEETLES

Although, as might be anticipated, both quality refinement and genuine specification development were singular by their absence, the relatively brief period between Hitler's defeat, the Nazi Party's annihilation and the advent of a new era in the first month of 1948 was incredibly important. Three equally significant, but nevertheless distinct, factors made this so.

First, the good fortune of the former KdF factory to fall within the British zone of occupation resulted in a young REME major being despatched to the now ownerless buildings with no specific orders other than to take charge. That officer, Ivan Hirst, proved himself not only to have complete faith in the Beetle as an ideal means of transport when many around him did not, but also to be an excellent improviser, an ability which made him ideally suited to manage the extraordinary circumstances surrounding the car.

Second, countries that might have laid claim to the component parts which made the Beetle capable of standing or falling on its own four wheels elected to ridicule its merits, condemning it, or so they thought, to wither and die, or worse still for its immediate well-being, to be axed at a single stroke.

Third, the determination of the British government that they didn't wish to control Volkswagen, but were merely custodians of German interests until such point that stability and growth was sufficient for the factory and car production to be handed back to them, would result in a staff appointment of uncapped merit. To withdraw effectively, ailing production figures had to be addressed, presenting a pressing need to strengthen the denuded and largely incompetent German management team. This decision resulted in the appointment of a former Opel director who had been eking out an existence as manager of a repair shop.

Fact not fiction – a doomed factory

The Beetle's story is so full of strange quirks of fate that if it were a work of fiction the author would be roundly condemned for the lack of authenticity in its plot. The opening scenario was one of impending doom at a time when comparatively few cars had been built, of which none had been distributed to the people for whom they were intended. As the end of the war approached and Hitler's troops faced certain defeat, the prospects for the KdF plant were decidedly grim, for three primary reasons.

First, and outwardly foremost, the once prestigious state-of-the-art factory bore signs of extensive damage, having been bombed on several occasions, the first raid in 1943 being followed by a series of more concerted attacks the following year. Near contemporary accounts referred in one breath to 'several thousand' incendiary devices being dropped on one occasion and in the next to what was described as a 'single high-explosive bomb', which had 'completely destroyed an assembly hall with a floor area of 861,000sq ft'. Certainly Hall Three lacked the majority of its roof, while Hall Four, the factory's machine shop, had been extensively damaged. However, as was later pointed out, the

Right: Major Ivan Hirst.

Left: Bomb damage at the former KdF factory was extensive, with some 60 per cent of the plant affected in one way or another.

damage was deliberately left unrepaired, while German soldiers had apparently been instructed to accentuate the damage by encouraging further sections of roof to fall in. What at first might appear a most unusual course of action in reality made a great deal of sense, as the factory's near-derelict appearance acted as a safeguard against further attack.

Secondly, the fabric of the factory was further imperilled when the maltreated workforce and the inhabitants of the associated shanty town realised that at last their hour had come. Higher-ranking personnel, including the Beetle's mentor, Ferdinand Porsche, were long gone; and as the days ticked by in April 1945 the last remaining representatives of Nazi officialdom also fled, having first destroyed their files, despoiled portraits of the Party hierarchy, and buried their now disgraced uniforms. Having suffered the most appalling of conditions, the one-time enforced labourers not unnaturally

Above: This rather dark image shows the shell of a Beetle against a background of rubble, the result of wartime bombing raids on the KdF factory. For the duration of British rule at Wolfsburg, production was hampered by war damage.

Right: In establishing a new era, Nazi designations of the factory and associated shanty town as 'Strength through Joy' (KdF) locations were swept away, with the very British Wolfsburg Motor Works sign taking pride of place at the factory entrance.

went on the rampage, ripping phones from the walls, scattering and burning records, sledge-hammering typewriters and carrying out similar acts throughout the factory. Their unorganised and volatile campaign extended into the town, where shops were looted and traders either shot or simply thrown out. A freight train temporarily abandoned in the KdF factory sidings was literally torn to pieces, its contents – other than a consignment of schnapps, which was rapidly consumed – strewn across a wide area.

Thirdly, there was the additional significant question of the KdF plant's ability to make anything at all, let alone the Beetle for which it had been built. Reasonably early on in the welcome process of the disintegration of the Reich, orders had come from Berlin for the transfer of the factory's facilities to mines at Longwy, near the borders of Belgium and Luxembourg, in order that they be protected from the increasing likelihood of air raids. One train carrying 200 machines had made the journey before the operation was aborted due to the mines being seized by the advancing Americans. Persuaded by those surrounding him to take whatever

action was necessary, the soon to depart Ferdinand Porsche rushed engines into a potato dehydration plant at Neindorf, front axles and steering axles into a barn at Fallersleben, motor parts into

forest barracks at Soltau, and the lighter machinery to Lüneberg. By April 1945 there was little left save the heavy presses, which by their very nature were almost impossible to move.

Above: Major Ivan Hirst (extreme right) with other members of staff outside the clearly bomb-damaged factory.

A glimmer of light

When the factory and town's liberation came on 12 April 1945, following the arrival two days earlier of an advance party of the 405th Regimental Combat Team from the US 102nd Infantry Division, few if any gave thought to another admittedly more political or academic reason why prospects for the factory were decidedly bleak. Due in part to the enduring intransigence of a German motor industry determined to preserve its own self-interests, it was the Nazi Party that had built the KdF plant. Now that the Party was to be banned forever by Allied decree, the factory and everything associated with it was ownerless and as such a prime target for destruction.

A series of catalysts – some major, some decidedly not so – saved Wolfsburg, as the factory and town were referred to from the moment of their occupation

(though official recognition of the name was only acknowledged by town officials on 25 May 1945). The first factor, which might appear relatively insignificant now, was of immense importance. Before the last creatures with allegiance to the Nazi regime deserted the KdF factory, two of their number planned to carry out an instruction of the deserting plant manager to blow up the canal bridges and destroy the factory power station. Hurrying to meet them, the town's acting mayor, Kurt Hofer, managed to persuade them – no doubt aided by a threat to call out the local militia – that the generators were the only source of electricity for the town. Meanwhile, Fritz Kunze, the director of the power station, proved dedicated to his duty and throughout the rioting the turbines ticked over. Without power, the factory's prospects would have been bleak indeed.

The Americans perceived their holding role to be one of asserting law and order, a task which extended to securing and enhancing food supplies, posting guards on the factory as part of a wider strategy of tight military security, and even to the appointment of the former factory chief inspector, Rudolph Brörmann, as plant manager. By mid-May 1945 the situation had stabilised sufficiently for some of the factory workforce to be given the task of repairing damaged US vehicles, while a few Kübelwagens were assembled from available parts. However, all such actions were anticipatory, as the area of land covered by Wolfsburg and the nearby village of Fallersleben fell, after negotiation between the Allies, within what had been designated the British area of control.

The British on board

The British arrived in mid-May, the first officer to set foot on Wolfsburg's soil being Colonel John Mackay. He had been briefed at Divisional Headquarters that the Red Cross had an understandably urgent need for transport. Meeting with Brörmann, the plant manager implied that the task of building vehicles and retrieving the necessary machinery from its various dispersal sites was an easy one, and so, beguiled by the rosy picture painted by Brörmann, Mackay arranged for 30 three-ton trucks to be driven to Wolfsburg, ready to carry out the task as quickly as possible. However, Brörmann's claims proved optimistic and although both a number of Kübelwagens and what might be loosely termed Beetles with military underpinnings were built from parts found in the factory, no great progress was made. Fortunately, despite this setback, the repair of military vehicles continued unabated, with a detachment of the Royal Electrical and Mechanical Engineers (REME) developing the process initiated by the Americans.

The REME unit was under the direction of Colonel Michael McEvoy, who was based at Rhine Army Headquarters, and although his part in the Beetle's story proved brief it was nevertheless an important one. Inherited wealth had given him the opportunity to establish McEvoy Racing Motorcycles before the war, and this operation later turned towards both special conversions on popular vehicles and to supercharging. During 1938, at the behest of Mercedes (for whom he was already acting as a consultant), McEvoy moved to Stuttgart and from there visited the 1939 Berlin Motor Show, where inevitably he came across the much-vaunted KdF-Wagen. Suitably impressed at the time, McEvoy was to prove instrumental in recommending the post-war Beetle to those with the power to decide its fate.

Various interpretations exist of what happened next. Those who had the good fortune to meet with Ivan Hirst during his years of retirement in his native Yorkshire will have heard from his own lips the story

Above: Major Hirst – at left, on this occasion without glasses – shows one of a regular string of visitors a Beetle assembled during the British period of occupancy at Wolfsburg.

Right: 1 March 1946 was the date when the 1,000th British-built Beetle was completed. Known as the Type 51, these cars featured a saloon body on the chassis of a Kübelwagen.

Opposite: Ivan Hirst can be seen quite clearly at the wheel of the 1,000th post-war Beetle.

The 1000th VOLKSWAGEN built during MARCH 1946 coming from Assembly Line

The **1000th** VOLKSWAGEN built during MARCH 1946 coming from Assembly Line

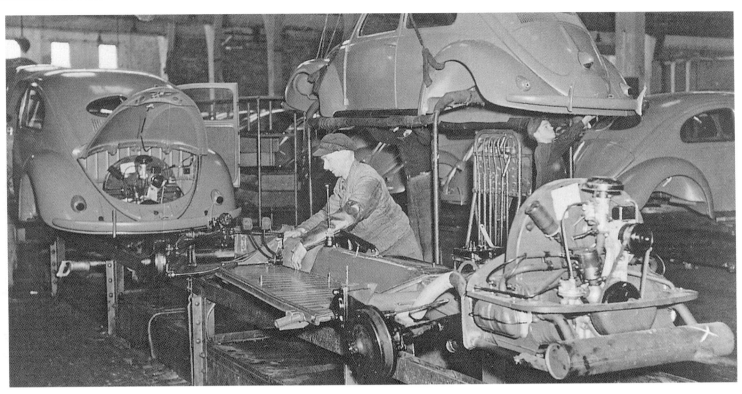

This spread: Wolfsburg's extensive archive of imagery of Beetle manufacture in the period of British control appears to suggest that working conditions were more than adequate, and that assembly problems were few and far between. Sadly, reality was somewhat different, with gaping holes in the factory's structure, machinery in desperate need of repair, a severe lack of tools, serious shortages of materials, a troubled workforce, and an ad hoc style of management.

of how he was sent to Wolfsburg in August 1945 'with no specific orders other than to take control of the former Nazi factory'. However, this statement oversimplifies the situation. If McEvoy had already advocated that car manufacture at Wolfsburg had a vital role to play in rebuilding Germany, Hirst was sent to Wolfsburg as a representative of the Military Government under whose remit such a task came, rather than as a senior officer whose job was to administer and develop the repair of existing vehicles of a variety of makes for the benefit of a hard-pressed army. A traditional view might be that the latter lurched towards the former almost by accident, due to two factors: Hirst's unique combination of genuine enthusiasm and inventiveness in the most trying

of circumstances, despite having only an amateur's understanding of the car manufacturing business; and the inability of the Military Government to dispose of Wolfsburg, if that was the intention, to any commercial or even political taker.

The view of Wolfsburg's official historians is somewhat different. Ralf Richter states in his biography of Ivan Hirst that the 'British army and military government did not see the Volkswagen Works primarily as a car factory. The Allies were convinced that there was no long-term perspective for the factory. Dismantlement prior to export was the plan – whether sooner or later.' This opinion undoubtedly stems in part from the declarations made by the Military Government on behalf of the Allies regarding German industry

in the British zone. However, even this is not straightforward, as for many years now Volkswagen has chosen to belittle the achievements of its first true director general, Heinz Nordhoff, in a complicated battle to prove that it was this man who nearly brought Volkswagen to its knees several years after his death. The title of Richter's book, *Ivan Hirst – British Officer and Manager of Volkswagen's Post-war Recovery*, an achievement credited universally to Nordhoff in his lifetime and by a reasonable percentage of authors to this day, acts as confirmation of the author's officially condoned belittling of the Nordhoff era in favour of a reinterpretation of British success. If, as Richter proclaims, the British intention was that Wolfsburg was to be wiped off the face of the earth, Hirst's

Right: Final assembly of Beetles in the early days.

achievement in saving it from destruction makes his part in the Beetle's story all the more significant.

Politics and interpretation

By unanimous agreement the policy of the British Military Government was that the German armaments industry was to be totally dismantled and that any country that had been at war with the Third Reich was entitled to bid for both capital equipment and machine tools of any type as war reparations. However, when the case of the Volkswagen factory was addressed matters weren't quite so simple. There was general agreement that Wolfsburg had been built for the purpose of manufacturing cars for civilians, primarily German, but in the

Left and below: Completed cars were generally despatched from Wolfsburg by train, but a smaller percentage were conveyed to their destinations on large car transporters.

Above: On 1 October 1946 the first standard saloon, given the Type number 11, came off the makeshift production line. A photographer was commissioned to take an official press photo.

longer term those from other countries as well. The KdF plant's subsequent war work hadn't been planned at the time of its conception. However, there was also the 'Level of Industry Plan for Germany' to take into account, a strategy designed to place a limit on Germany's post-war industrial activity. The policy document included reference to any factory not fully operational by 1938 as being a part of the Nazi war preparations effort, and as such surplus to requirements in the aftermath and as a consequence appropriate for inclusion as available for reparations.

In his account of his time at Wolfsburg written for the journal of the Royal Electrical and Mechanical Engineers in April 1962, the by then long retired Major Ivan Hirst stated simply that 'in view of the Occupation requirement for its product ... a four-year reserve was placed

on the plant'. What appears to have been the case was that Hirst was initially preoccupied with essential restoration work – the factory's plumbing and drains were both badly damaged and the latrines were more or less blocked. Hirst also had little option but to turn his attention to the provision of food for the factory's inhabitants. Essentially dependent on two farms situated locally, as the national supply chain was broken, Hirst arranged for the ground in front of the factory to be ploughed and turned over to the production of crops.

When the pressing combination of food and smells was under control, Hirst could occupy himself with surveys to find out just how badly the factory complex had been damaged, safe in the knowledge that the essential repair work to military vehicles was being carried out in an area

of the factory where bomb damage and neglect wasn't an issue. Heinz Nordhoff was later to portray the destruction as near total, although as proof that the words of the director general from 1948 onwards weren't anything more than an attempt by his PR team to rewrite history in his favour, the near-contemporary writing of one other writer is also worth noting, alongside Ivan Hirst's irrefutably conclusive statement. The motoring journalist K.B. Hopfinger, author of *Beyond Expectations*, the best-selling 1950s account of Volkswagen's post-war recovery, felt confident in writing that 'by 1944 more than 65 per cent of the Volkswagen plant lay completely in ruins'. This was based on his first-hand experience of frequent visits to Wolfsburg from 1946 onwards, when he was able to 'observe the reconstruction of the plant'.

Writing in the REME journal in 1962, Hirst's summary was similarly not open to misinterpretation: 'At the end of the war, then, we came to a more or less derelict works'. The sentences that followed only serve to elaborate on the feeling of desolation and finality that faced him on his arrival: 'Porsche had gone to Austria, later to be arrested by the French; the factory medical officer was ... condemned to death by a British Court, and hanged...'.

Volkswagen's latter-day chroniclers have chosen to rewrite history. Hall Three, they allege, suffered most with 68 per cent damage to its structure, but the overall level of destruction is now indicated to have been a surprisingly light 20 per cent. Crucially, the argument goes that 93 per cent of the machine park was reusable, although the funds and manpower weren't available to rebuild the damaged parts of Wolfsburg instantly. Perhaps

the revelation that Hirst ingeniously instructed that tarpaulins supported by pine tree trunks should be slung across the gaping holes in the nucleus of the factory, the press shop, reveals more than some would like to admit. Fortunately for the Beetle, however history is interpreted, thanks to Hirst's improvisation approximately two-thirds of the complex became usable relatively quickly – at least when the weather was clement.

Backing the Beetle

Colonel McEvoy knew exactly what should happen if the *Volkswagenwerk* was to be of genuine benefit to the Allies, albeit on an interim basis. Demand for transport by the military (and not just the British forces) was immense. To utilise Wolfsburg for such purposes, thus providing what was required without cost to the hard-pressed British economy and taxpayer, was ideal. Logically at this stage the vehicle to revive was the highly versatile Kübelwagen, but fate was to play a crucial card.

Before the war Porsche had gone on a discovery tour to America, and as a part of his busy schedule had visited the Budd Corporation. Here he negotiated the right under licence to make an all-steel body for the Volkswagen utilising the Budd procedure. In return, he agreed that Budd should have the right to make the bodies for the first Beetle-based derivative, naturally assuming that this would be the low-volume cabriolet version of his car. At the outbreak of war America was not a participant, and Budd had no qualms in insisting that they produce the bodyshells of the military orientated Beetle derivative, the Kübelwagen, at their Berlin-based sheet metal press works, which traded under the name of Ambi Budd. By the war's end the factory in Berlin was so badly damaged that little remained, although one or two dies for the Kübelwagen pressings were found. Although these wouldn't have made production complete, a further obstacle to the reincarnation of the Kübelwagen existed: the Ambi Budd factory lay in the Russian zone, and it soon became clear that it would be impossible to retrieve what was needed.

Without the Kübel, attention turned to the saloon, and at McEvoy's behest Hirst located one of the few Beetles to have been built at the beginning of the war, had it resprayed in Khaki Green and despatched to HQ, where the experienced Colonel demonstrated it with great skill to colleagues both within the ranks of the British Army of the Rhine and the Control Commission for Germany, the CCG. Under the Level of Industry Plan the quota for car production in the British zone was set at 20,000 vehicles. (In the American zone the total figure was the same, but divided between two manufacturers, 15,000 being allocated to US-owned General Motors' satellite Opel, with the balance of 5,000 cars going to the Daimler-Benz factory. There was no allocation agreed for either the French or Russian zones.) The Ford factory had been declared the designated manufacturer in the British zone, but at the time the Beetle was presented it was many months if not years away from recommencing production, despite a limited ability to meet the military's need for trucks. As such, the way was open, at least on a temporary basis, to allow Wolfsburg to supply cars. McEvoy's persuasive argument that by employing Volkswagen the British sector's economy would be revitalised clinched the order, with the CCG requesting 5,000 Beetles initially, only to increase that number to a 20,000 commitment shortly afterwards.

Fate played a further hand in the Beetle story in the form of the steadying and undoubtedly expert hands of Charles Radclyffe. A veteran of both world wars, where he had served theoretically as a tank

engineer but in reality as an expert, the Colonel had been appointed head of the Military Government's light mechanical industry division at Minden. As such Ivan Hirst had as his immediate superior a knowledgeable automotive professional, someone who in peacetime had acted as the White Truck Company's representative in both the Far East and India, before returning to Britain, where he became a sales executive for Alvis. Radclyffe proved to be the steadying hand to Hirst's overenthusiasm, and while he might sanction the unnecessary development of a forerunner to Volkswagen's – and more particularly Hebmüller's – short-lived Beetle coupé by an underemployed developmental department, more major issues that might have affected the Beetle's wellbeing were considered with all due caution. One such project was the proposition first concocted on the leaf of a pocket notebook by extrovert Dutchman and would-be Beetle importer Ben Pon. His proposal, later to become one of the most famous of all, was that Volkswagen should diversify with the introduction of a small commercial vehicle, which inevitably Pon would import and make a pretty packet out of. Hirst's immediate reaction to Pon's plan was one of typical schoolboy enthusiasm with little or no consideration for the consequences of falling Beetle production numbers against what should have been an improving background. Radclyffe was the calming influence with regard to such whimsical notions, but as Ivan Hirst told the author a few months before his death, nevertheless commanded his respect as 'a wise old guy' throughout.

The art of improvisation

Below: The 10,000th Beetle stumbled off the assembly line in October 1946. Official photographs heralded the occasion as a great success. The image reproduced here paints a rather different story. Apart from a list of requirements that included a decent meal and a pint of beer, the plaintive cry of '10,000 cars, but nothing to eat, can we bear it?' remains something of a shock.

Interviewed by Karl Ludvigsen, author of *Battle for the Beetle*, Ivan Hirst spoke of the factory's big presses being repairable, but also of new assembly jigs and welding equipment having to be made. Similarly, following the abrupt closure of the factory making crankcases and transmission housings (due to the majority of its business having been associated with the aircraft industry, which was now summarily curtailed), Hirst had little option but to open a foundry. While such revelations indicate his ability to improvise, perhaps they also give a hint of the amateur's enthusiasm to gamble with the operation's future.

Inevitably, in the building of those first cars shortages arose. Ad hoc solutions, feats of improvisation, were the hallmark of the time. For example, Hirst wrote many years later of the lack of sheets of steel large enough to create the Beetle's roof panel, and how he had ordered a butt welder to be designed and built at Wolfsburg, so that one large sheet of steel could be created out of two smaller ones. This tale, recounted in his REME journal article in April 1962, has often been queried as an elaboration of fact into fiction. However, a vehicle exhibiting the signs of such methodology has recently emerged, confirming that this and other stories are entirely credible.

To the author's delight, a day spent with Ivan Hirst encouraged many stories in a similar vein, sufficient in number for them to be worked into an article, which was subsequently checked by Ivan for authenticity and a lack of literary embellishment.

On one memorable occasion it was brought to Hirst's attention that only three weeks' stock of carburettors remained. As they had been made by Pierburg in Berlin, to a Solex design under licence, it was clear that an alternative source of supply had to be found. Hirst proceeded to strip one of the remaining examples down on his desk, dividing the components into those that could be made at the factory and those that couldn't. The smaller brass parts were duly taken to the nearby town of Brunswick and to the camera firm of Voigtländer, which agreed to recreate items such as the float and the jets. Meanwhile, the carburettor body and fuel chamber were developed at Wolfsburg as gravity die castings worked in aluminium. Concluding the story with a theatrical filling of his customary pipe, Ivan's punchline was that the Wolfsburg-manufactured and assembled carburettors lacked the expected Solex stamp!

Such ad hoc solutions to shortages perhaps inevitably led to unfortunate consequences. For example, due to the lack of a suitable adhesive, fish glue had been sanctioned to fix cloth on to the door panels. The resultant odour when such cars were driven in the rain was truly appalling. Similarly amusing is Ivan Hirst's recollection of the use of cardboard to insulate the battery terminals from its pressed steel cover. Inevitably, by its very nature it soon rotted away when exposed to acid fumes emitted by the battery. A spring was used to hold the battery cover itself in place and if this came into contact with the positive terminal it heated up, acting like the element of an electric fire. As a result, female rear-seat passengers could easily find that holes had appeared in their stockings!

Potentially far more serious were the steering-arm drop forgings that fractured in service. Subsequent investigations revealed cracks, and despite testing by a War Department crack detector the problem persisted. The fault lay at the door of the suppliers, who, embarrassed by the shortage of steel, had taken to recycling rejected forgings by welding them and then disguising their actions by striking them under the drop stamp for a second time.

In fact the lack of the necessary materials coupled to tooling shortages and worn machinery was sufficient to lead to a catalogue of misdemeanours, examples of which were: doors, engine lids, and boot lids that failed to shut properly; headlamp lenses that cracked when the

vehicle wasn't in motion; and even glove-box compartment liners that curled up uncontrollably.

Enduring problems were experienced with the Beetle's finish. Issues ranged from a single batch of cars produced in November 1946 that were coated in such heavy layers of dust during assembly that the paint process was blemished, necessitating a respray, to ongoing issues of rusting on the door hinges, the flanges on both the engine and boot lids, and the rain channels on the car's roof. However, the most common complaint of all from customers – including military governments – was disappointment at the lack of a high-gloss finish, while liming and general unsightliness resulted in an unacceptably high percentage of resprays well into the latter months of 1947. The British Beetle, at first acceptably makeshift, continued to demonstrate a standard that would have been unacceptable in earlier years and, as other manufacturers regained their feet, would inevitably become so once again.

The diversion of an officer's game

A visit to Wolfsburg by Michael McEvoy in the early months of 1946, armed with a wild idea for production of a mid-engined Beetle with an aptitude for racing, caused something of a stir in the office of Ivan Hirst. Although he rejected McEvoy's idea with the eminently practical reply that he was unable to keep pace with Allied demands for cars let alone take on a new project, a spark of interest was ignited that led to the production of a prototype strictly for officers and gentlemen and, however entertaining, an unnecessary red herring in the battle for survival.

An ebullient Hirst turned to his tiny developmental department and suggested they create a two-seater cabriolet based on the Beetle. The distinct lack of enthusiasm with which the project was received, largely due to the amount of panel beating involved, spurred Hirst to suggest that a modified Beetle bonnet would make an ideal engine cover. Within a few weeks the car was ready, although no plans existed to make

use of it by furthering its design towards series production. The one-of-a-kind was presented to Colonel Radclyffe for use as a summer plaything, even being nicknamed the 'Radclyffe Roadster' as a result, while at other times Ivan Hirst revelled in its use at weekends. As it was officially the property of the Volkswagenwerk, when the vehicle was damaged in an encounter with a steel girder it was repaired at Wolfsburg. The experimental department was at liberty to recall it at any time if further entertainment was planned, as indeed they did when, in an unsuccessful move to endow the vehicle with extra power, twin carburettors were fitted.

In the end the Radclyffe Roadster served a genuine purpose, although this hadn't been planned by Hirst when he commissioned it, as it gave Josef Hebmüller the idea for his Beetle coupé which was destined to go into production in 1949. Sadly, it also came to illustrate the spirit of the British era and the lack of professionalism embodied therein.

Below: On 16 October 1947 Ben Pon (second from the right) took delivery of the first Beetles to be exported. There should have been six cars, but one failed the necessary inspection process.

Misguided judgement of the experts

Fortuitous as it would prove for Germany and Volkswagen in later years, and despite British Armed Forces and Control Commission satisfaction with the Beetle, not to mention the REME Inspectorate's conclusion that the car's basic design was sound – 'many of the inevitable "bugs" … [having] been eliminated during production of the open car for the German Army' – a barrage of experts and reports from influential bodies confirmed to those with designs on Wolfsburg's assets that the factory contained little of value.

Best remembered of the many insults heaped on Porsche's creation are those of William Rootes, who on a visit to Wolfsburg told Hirst that if he thought he was going to get cars built there he was

nothing more than a 'bloody fool'. The commission of which Rootes was head reported that the Beetle did not 'meet the fundamental technical requirements of a motor car. As regards performance and design it is quite unattractive to the average motor-car buyer. It is too ugly and too noisy … a type of car like this will remain popular for two or three years, if that. To build the car commercially would be a completely uneconomic enterprise.'

One highly detailed assessment by Humber Engineering was based on their dissection of a Kübelwagen, but they did take into account differences in the form of the bodies, plus hub reduction gears and 'special tyre equipment and wheels' on the military version compared to the saloon.

The summary conclusion set the tone for subsequent reports, including further assessments carried out by the same company: 'We do not consider that the design represents any special brilliance, apart from certain of the detail points, and it is suggested that it is not to be regarded as an example of first class modern design to be copied by the British industry.'

Assessing a Beetle built when jurisdiction at Wolfsburg had transferred to the British, Humber said of the car's engine that it was 'somewhat noisy and rough', although while 'performance was by no means outstanding', petrol consumption figures were presentable. Although steering on bends was 'distinctly tricky' and the car had 'a tendency to over-

Production numbers

In the few months of 1945 available for car production Wolfsburg saw a grand total of 1,745 Beetles roll off its assembly line – a very creditable figure considering the chaos in which the plant remained for most if not all of this period. Apart from the essential work of builders and plumbers already referred to, bulldozers were required to fill in numerous bomb craters. The clearance of rubble from the roadways, aisles, and even the railway sidings was similarly important, while removal of all traces of the plant's wartime activities had to be a priority, if for no other reason than the presence of aircraft parts being a constant reminder of an unsavoury past.

Seemingly straightforward clearance work continued throughout 1946 and no doubt hampered the progress of car manufacture accordingly. The initial British target for Beetle production had been set at a very optimistic 4,000 cars per month by January 1946, but had to be hastily revised. By contrast, in early 1947 it was anticipated that production would reach 2,500 cars monthly by the end of the year. Although that target too was missed as realisation began to dawn that professional managers were

required if Volkswagen was to make real headway, the results produced in 1946 were sufficient to instil confidence in those with the power to determine both the car's and the plant's future.

Amidst a suitable degree of pomp and ceremony, the first time that 1,000 cars had been built in a month was duly recorded in March 1946. (The eagle-eyed would, however, have noted that parts shortages resulted in the most unusual of headlamps being fitted.) From that point on the monthly figure remained roughly constant for all but December of 1946, with the result that an encouraging 10,020 Beetles were built during the year, and the magical 10,000 barrier in terms of total post-war production was achieved in mid-October. By fulfilling at least in part the orders for cars it had received, the factory was granted firm contracts for a further 40,000 cars by the CCG, while permission was granted for the establishment of a sales organisation within the British zone. With effect from the Hanover Trade Fair of 1947, the Beetle was not only officially available on the home market, but it could also be exported. Sadly, despite these moves, production fell in 1947, so that just 8,987 cars were produced. A prolonged winter shutdown

at the beginning of the year hadn't helped, while material shortages did little to assist Hirst and his team meet the struggle of demand outweighing supply.

In July 1947 the British Property Control authority declared that 'the vehicles produced at the Volkswagenwerk have become a fundamental part of the transport position of all the occupying powers and therefore the production is mandatory in every respect'. Nearly a year earlier the directive that had pronounced the strategy for dismantling the former KdF factory had been put on hold for four years. A month later, in September 1946, the level of industry plan was revised, removing the restriction on the number of vehicles produced on German soil to an annual figure of 40,000.

As the Volkswagen factory now had a guaranteed future, and those with any right to take part or all of it away from Germany had rejected the Beetle out of hand, something had to be done. The British authorities recognised the urgent need to strengthen the management structure through the appointment of someone with technical expertise as deputy manager.

steer', this was nothing when compared to Humber's criticism of Porsche's much-lauded independent torsion bar suspension. Describing it as 'hard and choppy' at best and as giving 'a very poor account of itself' over both 'rough and smooth surfaces', the report writers stated that in their opinion the suspension was 'of a very poor standard for a civilian vehicle'. Driver vision wasn't necessarily restricted by the diminutive panes of the split rear window, but the 'thick and steeply curved windscreen pillars cause[d] a very serious blind spot'. A lengthy explanation of the Beetle's heating system was brought to a close with a brief notice of its admirable nature 'in many ways' being spoiled by both 'smell and fumes' from the engine.

Redemption came at least in part in the report's section devoted to the Beetle's body: 'It is our considered opinion that from the Body Engineering point of view the design of this vehicle is exceptionally good', it said. Unfortunately British prowess at Wolfsburg didn't receive a similar accolade. 'Workmanship and general finish of the vehicle leave much to be desired and could be improved ... No adequate measures seem to have been taken either for cleaning and de-greasing the pressings before priming, or any steps taken for rust-proofing...'

AC Cars' impressions were singularly damning: 'from the general construction one gets the impression that the designer has given just enough but no more ... as a civilian vehicle considerable modification would be required to conform to the standard expected'.

One by one all who had expressed even the vaguest interest in Wolfsburg and its sole product shied away from it. Henry Ford II was alleged to have said that he would not have the Beetle or the rights to it as a gift; reality suggests that the plant's proximity to the border of East Germany was the real reason for his dismissal of any interest. Australia had sent a small team over to look at the plant but took no further interest. An interest from France's Communist minister of industry likewise came to nothing, other than 50 cars being supplied for evaluation.

A way forward

As Hirst and his colleagues tinkered with production and enjoyed the cut and thrust of daily survival, while at the same time generally overlooking the lack of progress in developing sales, an altogether more dour figure in the shape of Berlin lawyer Hermann Münch acted not only as custodian of Wolfsburg's assets in the absence of a legal owner – a role bestowed upon him on 17 June 1946 – but, with effect from 1 August, as *Generaldirektor* too.

The original plant manager, Rudolph Brörmann, had been a victim of a second wave of de-Nazification programmes held during the first half of 1946, designed to cleanse Germany of those who had held positions of responsibility under the regime, or who could be exposed as having been sympathetic to the fascist cause. Brörmann's knowledge and understanding of the motor trade failed to save him against a barrage of union intrigue brought about by his dictatorial management style and highly suspicious mindset, and a consequent lack of desire on anyone's part to defend his achievements. Evidence exists that even Ivan Hirst did little to shield Brörmann, verification arising out of the tale of an argument between the two men concerning lack of progress on a car being built especially for Colonel Radclyffe.

Münch's press ranges from the noncommittal to the more openly unsympathetic, but virtually without exception there is recognition that the

Below: Dr Hermann Münch came to Wolfsburg as the factory's custodian and general manager. A lawyer by profession, and with a background in banking, Münch lacked experience in any manufacturing industry, and car production was an alien business to him.

lawyer's lack of expertise would have jeopardised the future of a Volkswagen quasi-independent of British control. Karl Ludvigsen in his book *Battle for the Beetle* aptly describes Münch as 'more necessity than asset'. Walter Henry Nelson, the doyen of authors in the era of the Beetle's supremacy, condemned the lawyer as being 'not much interested in the car or its future'. Münch, Nelson sneered, 'did not understand the car business and presumably cared little for it'. Although the ever-gentlemanly Hirst suggested that Münch was good in respect of both legal and financial matters, when interviewed in 1996 he had little option but to admit that neither the lawyer 'nor one or two people who came with him had the know-how or technical expertise to run a major manufacturing company'. Münch lacked an awareness of the practical difficulties in production, was oblivious to disorder and uneconomic practices, incapable of monitoring vital money-earning repair work, and, above all, had little or no experience in generating growth through sales.

Clearly, if the longer-term aspiration was for the Volkswagenwerk to emerge as a powerful force in the car manufacturing industry, capable not only of satisfying the demands of its home market but also of attaining realistic sales levels and much-needed revenue from exports, the management team had to be strengthened with both genuine technical expertise and far-reaching experience in driving sales forward. Münch was both unworthy and incapable; Hirst's star had shone brightly, but his lively amateur performance, so

Right: The so-called 'Radclyffe Roadster', an open-top model presented to Hirst's commanding officer, Colonel Charles Radclyffe, epitomises the period of British control. Hirst had the idea of building a two-seater cabriolet based on a standard saloon and set the experimental department the task of building such a vehicle. When the department expressed a reluctance to progress the project due to the amount of panel beating involved, Hirst suggested that they modify a Beetle bonnet. Some good came out of the oddity in that Hebmüller were aware of the roadster and based their coupé on the concept.

successful in times of ad hoc adversity, precluded guaranteed results as the factory moved towards settled, ongoing survival. As 1947 mellowed towards autumn it was also becoming increasingly clear that it wasn't and never had been Britain's plan to remain in control of a German factory, a German people, and a German government. Something had to be done for the Volkswagen and had to be done fast.

At the time, Heinz Nordhoff's interview and appointment lacked any form of controversy, pundits recognising that the time was right to lift Volkswagen's game from amateur to professional status, and that the talented, experienced ex-Opel man was the ideal person for the job. Only a bitter Münch's resignation suggested that peace and harmony wasn't completely universal. Nowadays, however, any discussion of this era centres upon Volkswagen's rewriting of history, as indicated earlier. Fellow author to Richter, Markus Lupa, again paid by Volkswagen to write historical notes at the behest of the Corporate History Department within Volkswagen AG, chorused his colleague's words in the volume entitled *The British and Their Works*. His book sets out to proclaim that it was 'British achievements in setting up a non-military automotive production plant in Wolfsburg' that precipitated 'the Volkswagenwerk's meteoric rise, which company folklore had previously attributed to the efforts of general manager Heinrich Nordhoff alone...'. The following chapters will allow each and every reader to decide for themselves, but for this author at least, Nordhoff became the Beetle and the Beetle became Nordhoff – the most successful partnership in the entire history of auto manufacturing and the motor car.

Starting his working career at BMW as an aircraft designer, Heinz Nordhoff soon graduated to Opel, which by 1929, when he joined them, was already a part of the vast General Motors Corporation. First employed as a department head within the service organisation, Nordhoff soon became a technical consultant to the company's sales managers. During the 1930s he was invited to America on several occasions to study General Motors' production methods. His meteoric rise

resulted in his appointment to the Opel board of management in the latter years of the decade, and in the early months of 1939 he transferred to Berlin to direct Opel's operations from there. Just over three years later Nordhoff was appointed director general of the Brandenburg factory, then the largest lorry plant in Europe.

Throughout his career his creed had been one of incredibly hard work, often resulting in committing himself to both weekend and holiday period endeavours to complete the tasks in hand. That Nordhoff was available for interview when called upon in the autumn of 1947 was a result of his holding the rank of *Wehrwirtschaftsführer*, an honour bestowed upon him by the Nazis despite his lack of Party membership. De-Nazification rules in the American zone where Opel operations lay had demanded Nordhoff's dismissal, and as a stopgap he had taken employment with the widow of the owner of the Hamburg-based Opel dealership, Dello and Co. So impressed was Hirst by Nordhoff's 'eminent suitability' at an initial meeting spanning two days of 'interviewing, walking round the factory and talking' that he recommended Colonel Radclyffe should appoint the 48-year-old not simply for a technical role but as general manager, ousting Münch in the process. On 7 November 1947 probably the single most important act in the Beetle's history was performed with the appointment of Heinz Nordhoff as director general of Volkswagen, a post he took up officially on 1 January 1948. With immediate effect Hirst and his

colleagues retired to a background role – Nordhoff had insisted on it.

Above: Former Opel director Heinz Nordhoff officially joined Volkswagen on 6 January 1948. Although he had impressed Hirst and others at his interview, few if any realised the impact he would have on the Beetle.

And the Beetle?

The era of British control was a non-event as far as the Beetle's development was concerned. Yes, changes were made to the peripheries of the design of the cars proudly paraded across Germany in the final year before the war, but those that occurred were the result of expediency. It was a question of utilising what was available – which led to charges of a lack of mechanical longevity and indifferent finish, both externally and internally. Compromise and improvisation were the

order of the day. The addition of a little tinsel and polish on a few cars in 1947 to launch the Beetle to a wider market was only successful because of the incredible demand for anything on four wheels in transport-starved Europe. Nordhoff became painfully aware of this within weeks of his appointment; his manufacturing expertise was desperately needed if Volkswagen and its sole product were to become professional players on the automotive stage.

1949–1953 EXPORT MODEL BEETLES

When Heinz Nordhoff addressed assembled journalists in 1954 his message was extraordinary in its individuality. Would any other company at that time, or at any other, consider the creed he advocated on Volkswagen's behalf? His strategy was diametrically opposite to a basic principle of motor manufacturing – the sacrosanct belief that only by constantly bringing out new models skilfully styled to catch the spirit of the age could a company strive towards the higher pinnacles of success.

'We are certain that the key to success lies not in the design and manufacture of daringly wonderful new products,' he declared, 'but in consistently and determinedly refining even the tiniest details until maturity and perfection are reached. This is what brings truly breathtaking success.'

Fourteen years later and just a few months before his death, Nordhoff remained unequivocal in his enduring belief in the Beetle as the lynchpin in Volkswagen's continuing success story. Although the car's design was now over 30 years old the director general saw no merit in casting it aside, whatever others thought.

'The star of the Beetle is still shining with undiminished brightness and you see for yourselves every day what vitality there is hidden in this car which has been pronounced dead more often than all those designs of which hardly a memory remains...'

Nordhoff's dogged determination to make Volkswagen the market leader not only in Germany and Europe but, it must be emphasised, with remarkable speed in nearly 140 countries across the world, and to perfect that model rather than replace it with another every few years, are among the fundamental reasons why the Beetle qualifies as a great car, the most-produced single model of all time. Heinz Nordhoff's campaign strategy began with the arrival of a new breed of Beetle, the De Luxe or Export model, in the summer of 1949.

Right: The 1949 Export or De Luxe Beetle, externally identifiable by its chrome bumpers, door and boot lid handles, and headlamp trim. Brightwork trim on the boot lid and along the car's sides were similar distinguishing features.

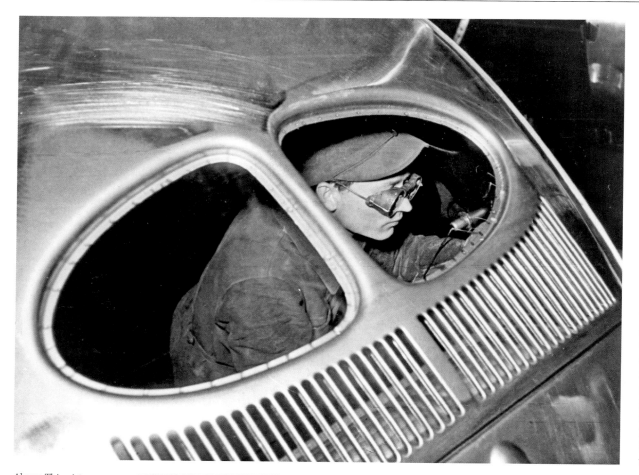

A heap of rubble and an ugly duckling

At the time of his appointment Nordhoff was singularly unimpressed with Wolfsburg's sole product. In November 1958, when accepting the prestigious Elmer A. Sperry award, an honour bestowed from time to time by three American engineering societies on individuals or bodies who had made significant contributions in the field of transport, Nordhoff recounted that the Beetle he inherited 'was still "full of bugs". It really was what you call an "ugly duckling".' On other occasions his message was the same: the Volkswagen, Nordhoff variously exclaimed, had 'more flaws than a dog has fleas', and was easy to condemn as 'a small, cheap thing'. The car was unacceptably noisy, exhibited extremely low standards of both paintwork and interior finish, and lacked mechanical reliability. In terms of saleability it was dangerously basic and offered little potential to all but the most desperately transport-starved of home-market buyers. Its specification was inconsistent, mostly but not entirely due to material shortages, while there had been no attempt to try

Above: This picture showing work on the assembly line in 1949 epitomises the era of the split rear-window Beetle, the car Nordhoff was determined should become a symbol of Germany's post-war economic revival.

Right: Two years into Nordhoff's reign as director general a great deal of repair work had been done. The picture shows the factory front in 1950.

Far left: The Wolfsburg press shop, photographed in 1950.

Left: The assembly line, circa 1950.

to develop the car either bodily or mechanically. In essence, what Nordhoff was faced with some three years after hostilities had ceased was the pre-war KdF prototype with the addition of an upgraded engine courtesy of the military Kübelwagen.

However, Nordhoff's inherited problems didn't end with the car; that was only the beginning. Addressing an audience in Zurich in 1954 Nordhoff recalled how he was 'faced with a desolate heap of rubble, a horde of desperate people, the torso of a deserted town – an unstructured mass which had never had any organising principle, no factory organisation in the real sense, lacking a programme or any rational work organisation'. In summarising, he was brutal in condemnation of past practices: 'Something new had to be created because there was nothing there

and never had been anything to build on at all.'

In his Sperry speech, Volkswagen's director general delved further into the troubles of the 'wrecked' factory: 'I had to start from scratch in the real sense of the word. Seven thousand workers were painfully producing six thousand cars a year, provided it did not rain too much. Most of the roof and all of the windows of the factory had been destroyed. At this time, nearly three years after the end of the war, 109.6 men were required to produce one car per day. ... There was so much to be done. Weak points in the design had to be ironed out, bottlenecks in production had to be broken, and problems of material procurement, quality control, personnel had to be solved. There was no sales organisation ... and I was determined that, of all things, Volkswagen should have the best service in the world.'

Although not directly referred to in the Sperry speech Nordhoff also had to temporarily countenance the lack of a cost-accounting system. Under Hirst's rule it was evident that the cost of building a single car could only be estimated, while there was more than a suspicion that one vehicle built might cost considerably more or less than its predecessor and successor on the somewhat ad hoc assembly line.

Addressing the workforce in 1948 following the swift realisation that 'things could not continue this way' and that 'desperation and confusion' abounded, Nordhoff was brutally frank. 'For the first time in its history, the Volkswagenwerk will this year have to face the necessity of standing on its own two feet.' Past practices could not be allowed to persist, for 'if we continue in this manner we shall not continue for long. We must reach 100 hours per car.'

The dashboard of Beetles built before October 1952 was typified by two symmetrically presented, small but open glove-boxes. Standard models all carried a black three-spoke steering wheel.

A single instrument gauge recorded all the information essential to the Beetle's driver. The speedometer appeared to run backwards as can be seen in the photograph. De Luxe models were trimmed in ivory plastic, rather than black.

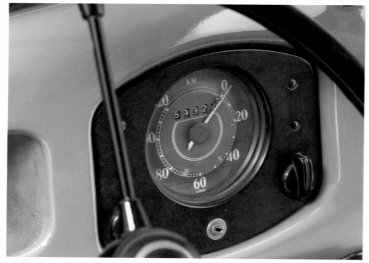

The horn on the Standard model of pre-October 1952 vintage was located behind the front bumper for all to see, unlike that on the De Luxe model, which was concealed behind the wing.

Although this car dates from the early 1950s, it is representative of the basic Beetle produced in the late 1940s to March 1953. Bereft of bright trim and lacking interior luxuries, this kind of austerity was inappropriate for export markets. Eclipsed by the introduction of the De Luxe model in June 1949, sales of the Standard Beetle steadily declined, cars of such a specification accounting for no more than 3.4 per cent of total production by 1960.

OSU 559

The early Beetle's diminutive 25PS flat-four air-cooled engine neither overheated nor froze solid; a definite, even definitive, selling point. Once perfected by Nordhoff's team, such engines were easily capable of 100,000 miles without major incident.

Two notes should always accompany such an image. The first relates to the Beetle's unusual roller-type accelerator, which was a feature of all cars built before the '58 model year. The second refers to the reserve fuel 'tap' (top right of the picture), a device required to offer drivers a further gallon of fuel when turned and vital in the absence of a fuel gauge. This device lingered into the 1960s.

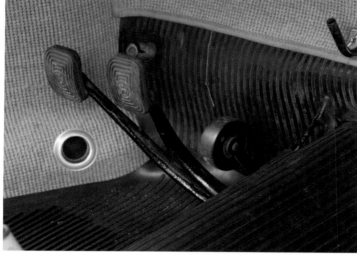

The Beetle's less than generous boot space was restricted by the prominent petrol tank. Note how the car could only be filled up with fuel by opening the boot lid!

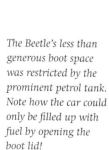

The split rear window characterised all Beetles built before March 1953. Curved glass was an expensive commodity, the science of its production being more or less in its infancy. Metalwork between two flat panes was a much cheaper option. In later years and for no particular reason, a split rear window Beetle was identified as the most visibly Germanic of all such cars.

Right: In keeping with the austere appearance of the rest of the car, the headlamp trims of Standard models were painted rather than chromed. However, the lovely domed shape would remain a feature of the car until the mid-1960s.

Far right: Similarly, door handles were painted on Standard models, and chromed on De Luxe cars. Note the coach-line, another characteristic of the base model, which in later years would be etched out in cream rather than the salmon pink shade in the photograph.

The De Luxe Beetle

One of Nordhoff's key actions in his drive to make Wolfsburg a 'decisive factor for Germany's peacetime economy' was the creation of two tiers of Beetle specification. The lineage of what might best be described as the British Beetle was refined to such an extent that although still basic in the extreme, at least its quality had improved dramatically, while an altogether more luxurious car, the De Luxe or perhaps more appropriately the Export model, was created that was altogether more palatable to all but native Germans with the most spartan tastes.

At least initially mechanically identical to the 'Standard limousine', the key to the success of the 'De Luxe limousine' was the considerable refinement in its trim specification. The Export model which had been in production from the beginning of June 1949 was launched during the following month, and almost immediately sales – or perhaps orders might be more appropriate – outstripped production, a situation that was to be perpetuated for more than a decade regardless of the ever-increasing level of investment ploughed back into the factory.

From the somewhat stagnant production figures of 10,020 Beetles built in 1946, 8,987 the following year, and 19,244 in 1948, numbers soon started to escalate. 46,154 Beetles left Wolfsburg in 1949, while in 1950 and 1951 respectively 81,979 and 93,709 cars were produced. More significant still was the steep curve in the graph of export sales. In 1949, 7,128 Beetles were sold outside Germany – a figure equal to 15 per cent of overall sales; the following year – which in reality was the first opportunity Nordhoff's Export Beetle had to make an impact – this figure had increased to over 30 per cent, a figure maintained over the next couple of years and from there on notably bettered, as the Beetle took America by storm.

The Export Beetle's specification was a straightforward story of a combination of quality trimmings and a greatly enhanced package of parts. Externally the Export model benefited from a comparative abundance of chrome, with bumpers, hubcaps, headlamp rims, and door handles finished in this way as standard. Previously there had been attempts to add a little dazzle and sparkle to the basic Beetle specification with the occasional appearance of chrome, but in general painted bumpers, hubcaps and the

The Beetle's basic profile remained the same throughout its lengthy production run and can be summarised as including a heavily sloping boot and engine compartment lid, separate bolt-on wings and running boards. It was this shape that led to the car which was originally officially referred to as the Volkswagen, or Type 1, becoming universally known as the Beetle; a term VW eventually adopted.

Far left: Painted hubcaps on the Standard model, chromed on the De Luxe. However, all cars benefited from the attractive domed shape of the wheel cover. Note how the VW roundel has been picked out in a separate colour.

Centre left: Pre-October 1952 Beetles carried a licence plate light cover of this style, which in enthusiast parlance is known as a Pope's Nose. Whatever the merits of such a nickname, the housing had a more important function, for it was also home to the car's single brake light.

Top right: Semaphore indicators were part of the Beetle package on cars for the European market until the '61 model year, although Americans enjoyed the benefits of 'modern' flashers from May 1955.

like had prevailed. These now became the exclusive preserve of the base or Standard model.

The Export model's specification also included nominal aspects of what might best be described as visual tidying and trinket adding, which at first glance might be regarded as an unnecessary waste of money, but in reality enhanced the car's appearance and hence its sales appeal. While the basic car continued to feature a large and undeniably visible bumper-mounted horn, the more upmarket Export model's horn was concealed behind the car's left-hand front wing. The addition of a delicate circular brightwork trim to mask a sound-enhancing hole in the wing, counterbalanced by a matching dummy in the opposite unperforated wing, ensured

Above: Although the earliest of the Nordhoff-era publicity material used black and white photography to sell the Beetle, it wasn't long before colourful artwork predominated. The image shown is taken from the back cover of a publication dating to late 1949 or early 1950. Compare the artwork here with the stylish offerings of Wolfsburg's best-known artist, Bernd Reuters, as depicted on pages 73, 95 and 102.

Right, far right and opposite: On 4 March 1950 the 100,000th Beetle rolled off the assembly line. A youthful-looking Nordhoff was on hand for the occasion – the first of many orchestrated by his PR man Frank Novotny.

a considerable enhancement of the car's frontal aesthetics. Similarly, the addition of an entirely non-functional boot-lid mounted solid cast aluminium 'V' over 'W' roundel added untold points in a tally of visual ratings, as did brightwork strips neatly tacked to the running boards, the waistline of its front and rear quarter panels, and the doors, plus the raised metalwork of the centrepiece of the car's bonnet.

Finally, looking at the car's external aspects, most contemporary observers would agree that the overall standard of paintwork finish was considerably better. Gone were the days of semi-matt panels; there was consistent allocation of more attractive colours to the Export model, while the Standard lagged behind with choices restricted initially to grey, black and, subsequently, grey and blue.

Inside, upgrading of the car's appointments was even more noticeable, verging on a transformation, and certainly guaranteed to appeal to the masses who would buy a car not for its mechanical durability or engine performance alone, but on the merits of its creature comforts. The Export model could be distinguished from its lowlier sister by a full headlining that enveloped the split panes of the rear window and extended in the same manner to meet with trim panels at either end of the rear seat. New to the specification was the addition of cloth grab-handles on the pillars behind the doors, a feature that was useful for rear-seat passengers when entering or leaving the vehicle. Likewise, the cloth upholstery offered on the trim panels, and particularly the front and rear seats, was of a better quality and even encompassed rear-seat bolster cushions in the style offered by manufacturers of luxury vehicles. (The essential earthiness of the average Beetle buyer was such that this particular upgrade wasn't necessarily welcomed with open arms, and within two years of their introduction bolster cushions had been summarily deleted, never to reappear!) Whereas the base model retained black fittings the De Luxe model was fitted with ivory-coloured items, something which, although taboo for many years now on the basis of despairingly restrictive health and safety guidelines, had the effect of enhancing the car's internal appearance. Ivory fitments

extended to door furniture, dashboard controls and gauge surrounds, the gear-knob, and, most strikingly of all, the three- or two-spoke steering wheel. Publicity shots of the Export model invariably depicted the car fitted with a dash-mounted clock, or possibly the luxury of a valve radio, while careful scrutiny of the two open glove-box surrounds revealed the addition of delicate brightwork trim.

Behind the scenes, the higher price tag of the Export model at 5,450DM compared to that of the Standard at 4,800DM was easily justified through the inclusion of items such as better soundproofing materials in the engine compartment and the substitution of spring-loaded adjusting handles in place of the Standard model's wing nuts to alter fore and aft front-seat movement, not to mention the addition of facilities to alter the rake of the backrests, and the inclusion of hard-wearing cord trim and embedded steel rails for more practical and durable luggage storage in the area behind the backrest of the rear seat.

Continual improvement

Before rushing towards the next landmark in the Beetle's progress it is necessary to appreciate the motives behind Nordhoff's decisions, and to illustrate how his managers, engineers, and designers became engrossed in the process of masking the continual improvements their director general propounded with enduring repetitiveness.

Nordhoff openly admitted that initially he had gone 'out on a limb', and had deliberately 'broken away from the beaten path' with the aim of 'doing something unusual but highly constructive'. Justifiably lengthy, the following extract from Nordhoff's Sperry speech of 1958 is the core of a philosophy that would endure for a 20-year period. Some have argued that Nordhoff's love affair with the Beetle was a means of self-glorification, a theory in part fuelled by Volkswagen's Public Relations department, which clearly developed the cult of the infallible director general and his equally unbeatable Beetle. Others, and particularly so after his death, have condemned Nordhoff for lack of vision

Right: Like other manufacturers, Volkswagen were eager to demonstrate their wares at the various motor shows, utilising increasingly sophisticated display techniques on their high-tech stands. This is part of the stand at the Frankfurt Show of 1951, the car if nothing else giving the date away through the ventilation flap visible in the front quarter-panel.

and for ignoring the need to move with the times – factors, so they argue, that could easily have brought Volkswagen to its knees in the 1970s. Both arguments are flawed, as Nordhoff's message illustrates:

'Offering people an honest value, a product of highest quality, with low original cost and incomparable resale value, appealed to me more than being driven around by a bunch of hysterical stylists trying to sell people something they really do not want to have. ... Improving quality and value steadily, without increasing price; improving wages and living and working conditions, without "passing the buck", in reverse, to the customer; simplifying and intensifying service and spare parts systems; building a product of which I and every other Volkswagen worker can be truly proud, and at the same time earning enough profit, under an economic system of free enterprise, to improve production facilities with the most modern equipment, to no small extent bought in this country, and thus increase production and productivity this year – these things are, in my opinion, an engineer's task. This ownerless and capital-less company has to live on its own. It is not in a position to issue new shares – it simply has to come along by itself, and, believe me, it does. I am convinced that there will always be a market in this world, which we are far from covering now, for simple, economical and dependable transportation and for an honest value in performance and in quality. I am convinced that all over the world ... there are millions of people who will gladly exchange chromium-plated gadgets and excessive power for economy, long life and inexpensive maintenance.

'So I have decided to stick to the policy that has served us so well. Based on Professor Porsche's original design, the Volkswagen of today looks almost exactly like the prototype model that was produced more than 20 years ago, but every single part of this car has been refined and improved over the years – these will continue to be our "model changes". This policy has required, of course, a great deal in the way of determination and courage, on the part of myself and the members of our organisation. But it has led to success, and there is no greater justification than success, as every engineer will agree.'

Below: At first glance the Beetles in the photograph appear to date from March 1953 or later. However, careful scrutiny of the front bumper, for example, indicates pre-October 1952 models. The photograph has been doctored to remove the division between the two sections of glass characteristic of such cars in order to make it appropriate for presentation to would-be owners of later models.

Above right: The occasion of the arrival of the 250,000th Beetle, which rolled off the assembly line on 5 October 1951, was duly celebrated in a formal assembly at Wolfsburg.

Above: Genuine enthusiasm for the product is more readily demonstrated when Nordhoff takes centre stage alongside the car.

In April 1950 an attempt was made to offer draught-free ventilation in the car's interior by introducing cut-outs in the tops of the glass in the wind-down door windows. At the same time, and of significance, the Export model's cable brakes were replaced with altogether more effective hydraulic brakes.

In January 1951 a further attempt was made to improve interior air circulation through the introduction of opening flaps in the front quarter-panels. In April a particularly attractive enamelled badge, bearing part of the coat of arms of the Schulenburg family – for generations the owners of the castle where the KdF factory had been built, and now commonly known as the Wolfsburg crest – was fixed to the boot lid above the handle and at the end of the central aluminium trim strip. At the same time a polished aluminium trim was inserted in the rubber seal surrounding the windscreen, in the process instantly lifting the car's frontal appearance, while behind the scenes the Export Beetle and the as yet unmentioned Cabriolet version of the Beetle benefited from double-acting telescopic shock absorbers in place of the previous rear single-acting lever type. In October 1951 the jacking points were strengthened.

A new Beetle – October 1952

As will become evident in ensuing chapters, landmarks in terms of significant changes in the Beetle's appearance or performance later became natural boundaries for authors and enthusiasts alike. Curiously, however, one of the most significant upgrades of the decade following the war is rarely alluded to as a defining date in the Beetle's history: the single act, some six months later, of removing the strip of metal dividing the two panes of glass that comprised the car's rear window completely overshadowed the milestone events of October 1952.

Externally, the Beetle's appearance was changed by the addition of 8mm brightwork inserts to all of its windows (a feature which had previously been restricted to the Export model's windscreen), while the door glass was spilt by the introduction of conventional quarter-lights to replace the less than satisfactory ventilation flaps of the previous 18 months. While the retaining strip between the now truncated main door window glass and the new and eminently useful quarter-light was chromed as part of the Export model's specification, it was painted in the Standard model. Trim on the running boards and various panels of the Export model was also redesigned, becoming chunkier and smooth in appearance, and lacking the rib of earlier days. The bumpers – chrome in the case of the De Luxe and painted with the Standard – were redesigned and became both heavier and wider, while the previous somewhat delicate centre indentation was deleted. The attendant over-riders, again pertinent to all cars, were upgraded to match the new bumper style. The clumsy, exposed bumper-mounted horn on the Standard model was hidden behind the left front wing, while the trim concealing a hole in the wing to make the horn more audible was altered, becoming both larger and oval in shape. The number plate light cover on the engine lid was redesigned, becoming shallower in appearance, the main reason for this being a reduction in its function, as the tail lights on the wings now combined the separate functions of reflector, brake, and rear light. Oval in overall design, the rear-facing lens housed the night light, while a lens shaped roughly like an upside-down heart on the top of the unit somewhat bizarrely housed the brake bulb. Finally, without listing the minutiae of the upgrade, the old-style vertical handle on the engine lid was replaced by a chromed or painted 'T' handle, which was also available optionally with a lock.

The car's stance appeared different too, as the size of the steel wheels was reduced to 4J x 15. The tyres were similarly smaller but, of equal significance, were fatter in profile, becoming 5.60 x 15 rather than the previous 5.00 x 16 specification.

Turning to the interior, the most obvious change was the introduction of a completely different dashboard, which although not as symmetrical made the car appear less Teutonic in style, despite an admittedly not uncommon reliance on metal rather than other materials in its construction. Gone were the two open glove-boxes and the inconveniently situated central speedometer and ancillary gauges. Now the speedometer was directly in front of the driver, while indicator and warning lights were built into the dial. The semaphore-style indicators were now operated by a column switch to the left side of the steering wheel, while functions such as lights, wipers, and even choke were presented as a series of ivory-coloured pull-out button switches on a slightly recessed panel below the centre section of the dashboard. With the benefit of hindsight the least clever part of the new layout was the positioning of the ignition key, which was also located on this panel, but at the furthest point from the driver and in close proximity to the front-seat passenger. In an age when it wasn't frowned upon to let children sit in the statistically most dangerous seat in any vehicle, small fingers could easily interfere with the key, with potentially disastrous results. The dash centre section was dominated by a large and attractive brightwork grille (painted on the Standard model), which masked the speaker for the radio where this was fitted. An ashtray, initially minus any form of pull handle, sat above the ignition switch, while the remainder of the dashboard was allocated to a glove-box, which for the first time came with a lid. The new style of dashboard would last until the summer of 1957, when, like the original design, it was

replaced with an even more attractive and symmetrically balanced layout.

Although at first glance minor in nature, other changes tended to be of the decidedly practical nature for which Volkswagen would become renowned. Broader demister vents by the windscreen, and relocation of the interior light from a position above the split panes of the rear window to a site above the left door pillar, can be cited as two particularly good examples, although even a redesign of the rear compartment ashtray in an age when smoking was the norm is worthy of mention.

Away from the visually obvious factors that would make the car either easier or safer to drive, features that would lead to improved performance were plentiful, although in the burgeoning tradition of continual improvement these changes could not be considered final, as a minor amendment in the form of a flame trap

on the felt cone air filter the following month would serve to demonstrate. Of the extensive list of behind the scenes improvements brought in with the revamp of October 1952, an increase from five to six leaf torsion bars with a reduced diameter of 24mm (down from 25mm) might be considered typical, as would an increase in shock absorber travel from 90mm to 130mm, and the replacement of the 26VFIS carburettor with a Solex 28PCI version. However, on a grander scale, apart from the wheel size already referred to, surely the most significant of all was the introduction of synchromesh on second, third, and fourth gears; a feature which in an instant made driving a Beetle much easier. (For those who cried that the skill had been taking out of driving the Beetle, the Standard model retained its crash box and would continue so to do for a further decade and more.)

Below: The assembly line pictured in 1952, the year when production broke the 100,000 car barrier in a 12-month period for the first time. 114,348 Beetles left Wolfsburg that year.

The press like the Beetle

Above: The 'new' De Luxe Beetle of October 1952 can be identified by chromed quarter-lights, sturdier chromed bumpers, decorative trim around the rear side-windows (and the split rear-window panes), broader bright strips on the running boards, and oval rather than circular front-wing trims.

Contemporary automotive journalists, who just a few years earlier tended to condemn the Beetle out of hand as a product tainted by Nazism, began to write about the Beetle with growing admiration; the further refinement of the car in October 1952 only added more five-star fuel to this campaign. In the opinion of a reviewer in *The Autocar* in early 1953:

'The car has been progressively refined, by the introduction of bigger tyres, softer suspension, bigger dampers and thermostatic cooling control, and the so-called export version, also sold on the German home market, now has bright exterior metalwork, ventilating panels in the doors, hydraulic brakes and a synchromesh gear box. The original austere conception is still maintained for those who want transport without frills, the standard model with an ordinary gearbox, mechanical brakes, simplified equipment and no exterior plating, being offered at a price DM 1,000 (£85) below that of the export model, which was recently made available for test in Germany...

'An additional attraction is the air cooling, which reduces cooling problems equally in the tropics and in semi-Arctic regions, for "air does not boil and does not freeze"...

'It is easy for any driver to obtain the best performance from the car, through the gearbox, which must be just about the sweetest on any inexpensive car made. The short, rigid lever works with the utmost precision, and synchromesh of exceptional efficiency operates on second, third and top gears. The synchromesh cannot be beaten...

'The clutch is smooth in action, with light pedal pressure, and it easily handled full-throttle gear changes during the acceleration tests ... Handling is really very good ... steering is light and direct ... a small turning circle facilitates parking ... suspension is exceptionally good for a small car ... the new softer torsion bars and the modified damper locations have considerably improved comfort without sacrifice of controllability ... The hydraulic brakes have good power for emergencies and stood up to hard use without fading. Maximum power is available with a moderate pressure on the pedal and the full independent suspension helps to ensure safe, quick stops on rough surfaces,

Money matters

Key amongst the many issues Nordhoff had to resolve when he inherited Volkswagen was a lack of funds. As has already been mentioned, there had been no cost accounting system in place before his arrival, and while this had been easily rectified it didn't in itself generate money but merely allowed Nordhoff and his senior managers to appreciate what funds were available, what was spent, and whether processes were financially efficient.

The German government, such as it was at the time, remained more or less oblivious to the Volkswagenwerk's existence, only finally becoming aware of its existence and significance at the point a few years later when Volkswagen had become the biggest taxpayer in Lower Saxony. Exploratory appeals to the banks were spurned in exactly the same way that rejection had met Ferdinand Porsche's requests for funds to develop his car before the Nazis became involved.

As we have seen, Nordhoff's solution to this potential impasse was the creation of a Beetle that would appeal to export markets both in Europe and overseas. However, two other developments not of Nordhoff's making played into the

director general's hand. The first, the great currency reform of June 1948, initially created a crisis of epic proportions at Volkswagen. Overnight the German nation saw 170,000 million old Reichmarks shrink to somewhere in the region of 10,000 million of the new Deutsche marks. Nordhoff's limited funds shrivelled accordingly, dipping to just 62,000 DM when the wage bill for Volkswagen's 8,000 or so employees amounted to between 300,000 and 500,000 DM. However, currency reform did achieve two basic goals in that it stabilised the economy and provided a suitable basis for growth.

In a similar vein – although Nordhoff chose not to take advantage of the scheme – American support in the form of Marshall Aid had the same result. Nordhoff was later to suggest that the second development was of even greater significance to Volkswagen. This came in the form of lifting the restrictions imposed on industry, and handed the impetus back to free enterprise. The wheels of the German economy began to turn once more, allowing Nordhoff to expand his second tranche of Export model sales through the home market. This general reawakening allowed Volkswagen to

develop the first stages of a distributor and dealer organisation. The birth of the export market and the regeneration of the home economy encouraged a steady dribble of funds towards Volkswagen's coffers, money that could be spent on bringing the factory back to a usable state and even to expand it. In excess of three million square feet of both plant and administration buildings were reconstructed; a further 400,000sq ft of space was created following a carefully planned movement of the assembly line under one exceptionally large roof, to the location where it had been planned to belong in the first instance. For all concerned, the best news of all (however frustrating it might have appeared to be) was that there was no stockpile of unsold Beetles – quite the reverse, as *Stern* magazine reported with undisguised glee: 'At the moment there is a waiting list of 15,000 for Volkswagens in Germany, and about 7,000 export orders are outstanding.'

The Beetle's popularity was finally established, and it was in anticipation of such a state of affairs that Nordhoff elected to subcontract if the opportunity for a niche market product appeared.

---

while quite a light pressure is sufficient in normal use...

'The driving position is good. The sloping bonnet gives exceptionally free forward vision ... The roller on the throttle pedal gives sensitive control and the placing of the pedals permits simultaneous use of brake and throttle ... Interior finish is neat, with metal areas painted in the body colour and cloth upholstery in harmonising shades. Everything fits nicely and there are none of those obvious concessions to low production costs which are a depressing feature of some low-priced cars...
'The Volkswagen is a roadworthy, robust small car, bred on the *Autobahnen* and in the Alps. It gives a good performance without effort. It is nicely finished, easy to maintain and backed by elaborate service facilities at fixed prices.'

A cabriolet diversion

Although popular legend perpetuates the myth that Nordhoff was strictly a one-car man, this wasn't actually true, virtually from the day he entered Wolfsburg for the first time. Against a background of involvement with Opel's commercial vehicle sector, Nordhoff wanted to offer Volkswagen's customers a multipurpose genre of Transporters which could act as a people carrier or a delivery van or, even better, fulfil both functions at once. Work started on the Transporter – the vehicle that would eventually eclipse even the Beetle in terms of enthusiast collectability – over a year before the launch of the Export model, and it was destined to make its press debut only four months after the De Luxe saloon. Sales would inevitably

never hit those forecast for the Beetle, but nobody thought of the Transporter as a niche market vehicle. Such was its encroachment into ever-increasing Beetle territory within Wolfsburg that by the mid-1950s the Transporter had to be given its own factory in Hanover. Annual production by that time was over the 60,000 mark and its contribution to Volkswagen's coffers unassailable.

Although Porsche's pre-war jottings had included designs for a Beetle-based van the diagrammatic plans depicted ungainly vehicles with little more than a garden shed unceremoniously dumped above the engine and rear panels of a suitably hacked-down saloon – amazingly, one or two prototypes of these monstrosities were actually made. However, when Porsche and his associates were more or less ready to present the Beetle to the world at the time of the factory foundation-stone laying ceremony, two further variations on the theme were presented in addition to the saloon or limousine. Of these, it took Nordhoff until the spring of 1950 to add a Beetle with a fold-back canvas sunroof to the Wolfsburg assembly line, covering both Export and Standard models, while the other variation, a cabriolet, was never produced in any of Volkswagen's own factories. Although a reasonable seller on the home market, the appearance of a sunroof model in, for example, Britain was a fairly rare occurrence. While this might suggest that Nordhoff was pandering to the whims of a niche market option, in reality the inclusion of a sunroof model on the assembly line didn't involve extra skills or dull the pace of production, as the premium of just 250DM on the price of an ordinary saloon at the time of the model's launch serves to indicate.

The same could not be said of a cabriolet version. While the British regime had seen experiments in the direction of open-top motoring, in practice such developments were reserved for high-ranking military personnel and, as with the saloon, no attempt was made to calculate whether such a car could ever be a profitable proposition for its maker. In the Nazi era an open-top KdF-Wagen was a useful propaganda tool – the Führer could be easily seen being chauffeured from location to location – while in the years following the war the prevailing gentleman's club attitude illustrates that the cabriolet was not a serious contender for construction, profitable or otherwise.

Nordhoff recognised that there was a limited demand for such a model and was fortunate that there were coachbuilders in Germany who were begging to take on board the considerable workload it involved. Subsequent year-on-year sales of the Cabriolet totally vindicate Nordhoff's decision to grant the construction of the four-seat Cabriolet to Karmann of Osnabrück, and what was essentially a two-seater Coupé to Wuppertal-based Hebmüller. The story of a fire in July 1949 and financial instability at the latter is reasonably well known, as is Hebmüller's eventual bankruptcy. Records vary as to just how many of the strikingly attractive Coupés were manufactured, each with their bespoke engine lids that mimicked and therefore balanced the look of the boot lid, the hood which when down disappeared neatly into the bowels of the car, and in many instances their striking two-tone paintwork. What is known is that Karmann muscled in and completed 12 vehicles at its own works after Hebmüller's demise, but a speculative conservative estimate suggests that no more than 696 such cars were built. Extant production records imply that Hebmüller's busiest month came after the fire, for in January 1950 125 cars were built, while before November 1949 the best month had resulted in no more than 39 cars. Such figures made a mockery of the whole Coupé exercise when compared to production at Wolfsburg, when even as early as the end of 1948 a Beetle was leaving the assembly line once every three and a half minutes.

Karmann Cabriolet production was similarly low when compared to that of the saloon. From a starting point of 364 cars built in 1949, production grew year on year until 1953, when at 4,256 cars there was a slight drop on the previous year's figure of 4,763. In the year when the millionth Beetle rolled off the Wolfsburg assembly line, Karmann produced 6,361 while

Left: A restored Hebmüller, lacking its characteristic early Beetle dainty bumper overriders, but featuring much later wing-mounted flashing indicators. Even so, the graceful lines of the two-plus-two Beetle coupé are clearly evident.

Wolfsburg's 1955 totalled just 14 vehicles short of 280,000. Nordhoff's strategy of farming-out Cabriolet production while retaining control of quality standards and handling all sales and marketing was clearly the correct way forward.

Production of either a cabriolet or coupé version of the Beetle would have been a nightmare for Wolfsburg. Both Hebmüller and Karmann faced problems of flexing when they worked on prototypes, despite the Beetle's separate chassis with its attendant substantial backbone. This was most noticeable in poor alignment of the doors after only a few miles of test drives, while windscreen glass would crack as the surrounding metal shifted with the movement of the car. The only way to counter this satisfactorily was to weld substantial box-shaped strengtheners under both sills, redesign the front quarter-panels and make the rear ones more ample, add hefty reinforcements round the door openings, include a substantial cross-member under the rear passenger seat, and insert a weightier panel above the engine lid. A unique windscreen surround, special frames for both the front and rear side windows – the latter incorporating a mechanism that allowed it to be wound down – and, of course, a nearly handmade hood fabricated out of layers of cloth and horsehair, complete with a genuine glass one-piece rear window, ensured that the Karmann Cabriolet took many hours to complete. Add into the equation the fact that Karmann took Beetles from Wolfsburg and unceremoniously cut them off at the waistline and it's easy to see that here was a labour-intensive product that, even with a somewhat inflated retail price, still cut into the margins Nordhoff would have wished to achieve.

By 1954, at a time when Nordhoff had been so successful that he had been able to reduce the price of the Beetle on more than one occasion, the Export model sold on the home market for 4,850DM and its more basic sibling, the Standard model, at 3,950DM, compared with the hand-crafted Cabriolet that notched up a total selling price of 6,500DM – a substantial 34 per cent more than the best-selling De Luxe Beetle and 65 per cent more than the Standard.

Left: With demand for the Beetle saloon soon to outstrip supply for many years to come, Nordhoff wisely allowed coachbuilders Karmann to take responsibility for the niche market Cabriolet, a model the coach-building firm would continue to build until production finally ceased in January 1980.

1953–1957 OVAL-WINDOW BEETLES

'The Volkswagen is a phenomenon not only because of what it is technically, but also because of what it has become commercially. It is simply not enough to design a great car. That car must be produced in enough numbers to matter and affect events. It must then be placed in the hands of an organisation energetic and imaginative enough to build a world market against enormous odds, and must then be entrusted to a global network of salesmen capable of turning it into a success. The man under whom all this was accomplished is Heinz Nordhoff.' – Walter Henry Nelson, *Small Wonder – The Amazing Story of the Volkswagen*, 1967.

One single act

Amazing as it might seem, the single act of taking a hacksaw blade to the strip of metal between the two panes of glass that made up the Beetle's split rear window, and in so doing creating a car known far and wide by the nickname of the 'Oval', transformed it from an efficient and decidedly matter-of-fact Teutonic product into the considerably more homely and curiously lovable spirit of a rapidly emerging golden age.

The first Ovals left the Wolfsburg assembly line on 10 March 1953, just over five months after the car had undergone its second radical overhaul since Nordhoff joined Volkswagen in 1948. Although, as might be anticipated, changes had been made to the specification in that short time, nothing of significance had occurred;

and in reality the creation of a rear window some 23 per cent larger shouldn't have been earth-shattering either, but it *was*, for a whole variety of different Beetle-orientated factors, all of which were linked back to a decision made during 1948.

Right: This image, more than any other, epitomises the advance made by removing the rib of metal between the two sheets of glass that had characterised the look of the Beetle since 1938. Less Germanic and more inviting, the oval-window Beetle came to act as the symbol of real expansion.

The public relations factor

With the Russians advancing on his home city of Prague at the end of the war, Frank Novotny – until then the owner of a successful import-export business – gravitated towards Wolfsburg, where after encountering the seemingly despondent Hermann Münch on several occasions, he offered to resolve the issue of frequent press attacks on the Beetle by providing information to the newspapers and generally handling public relations. Initially unpaid, on Hirst's advice Novotny developed what he had envisaged as a Press Bureau into a Public Relations office, and it was in his capacity as Wolfsburg's PR advisor that he was asked to show the newly appointed Nordhoff around the factory.

The two men formed an instant alliance with a common purpose: Nordhoff liked Novotny due to his open and frank American style of doing things, something the newly appointed director general had come to appreciate while working for General Motors-owned Opel; Novotny in turn saw in Nordhoff an incredibly hard-working, technically gifted, charismatic figure, capable of transforming both the Beetle and Volkswagen into market leaders. It became Novotny's life aim to crown Nordhoff king of Wolfsburg and in so doing engender a worldwide Beetle empire of devoted followers of the cult of the director general. Once he was personally satisfied with the product Nordhoff was only too happy to speak about the Beetle's endless merits, whether to one journalist or a crowd of thousands, and the painstakingly hand-edited, meticulously prepared scripts soon had even the most hardened cynic craning his neck so as not to miss a single word. Novotny was entirely successful in creating such a cleverly orchestrated aura around Nordhoff that his Wolfsburg workforce virtually worshipped him as a god, his ever-expanding network of dealers bowed and scraped to his every desire; and because all knew that his one concern was to generate Beetle sales and in so doing create wealth and unparalleled working conditions for all, the cult of the car and its director general continued to soar.

It was through Novotny, the original spin doctor, that Nordhoff's declared aim of making Wolfsburg and Volkswagen 'a decisive factor for Germany's peace-time economy' was made so much easier. Volkswagen's in-house magazine, *VW Information*, shadowed Nordhoff's every move. Like an earlier *Hello* magazine, it depicted Nordhoff at home, in his garden, on holiday, devoted pages to celebrate his birthday, and later even set aside a complete issue in honour of his achieving the landmark age of 65.

Novotny's skills reached the first of many zeniths with the arrival of the millionth Beetle during the 'oval' years, and demonstrated the science of PR at its most effective.

The path to the first million

Within less than four months of the introduction of the oval-window model the 500,000th Beetle emerged from Wolfsburg on 3 July 1953. To achieve this goal had taken a little over eight years of hard labour, and Nordhoff ensured that an appropriate reward for such dedicated service was granted to every member of the workforce, a decision that cost Wolfsburg a well-spent 2.5 million DM. In just over two years time on, 5 August 1955, the millionth car was manufactured. 1953 had seen a 32 per cent increase in Beetle numbers over the previous year and that total of 151,323 cars would be eclipsed in 1954 by a further boost of 34 per cent to 202,174 vehicles. The calendar year 1955 would end with 279,986 Beetles leaving Wolfsburg and a growing series of fledging assembly plants across the world, creating a substantial 38 per cent jump in annual production numbers. The boom was not self-perpetuating; this was a result of Nordhoff's vision for Volkswagen and for the Beetle.

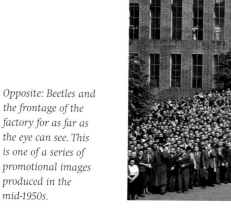

Right: Nowhere is the strategy of creating a regal figure out of Nordhoff, the father of the Beetle, more apparent than here. This image is one of a series taken as part of a planned feature in the press.

Opposite: Beetles and the frontage of the factory for as far as the eye can see. This is one of a series of promotional images produced in the mid-1950s.

Beetles abroad

Apart from the obvious implications surrounding the export of a total of 68,754 Volkswagens during the year – vehicles that raised an immensely useful 254.2 million DM with which Nordhoff could continue to build for the future – 1953 was a significant year in terms of prospective Beetle production numbers, for three major export players were either enlisted or provided with a much-needed boost during the course of the year. Of least significance was the establishment of a company devoted to selling the Beetle in Britain. Of longer, rather than immediate, consequence Volkswagen do Brasil SA was formed on 23 March, while after several years of struggling in the USA with a car that nobody seemed to want, Nordhoff took a decision of sufficient dynamism to electrify its future prospects.

The name of 'Export' model commonly bestowed on the De Luxe Beetle introduced in July 1949 provides an indication of Nordhoff's chosen direction for Volkswagen, a course that in fairness had already been advocated by the British Control Board, although their motive had been to an avoid the car costing the British taxpayer money. During 1948, at best ad hoc and at worst haphazard exports, possibly based on personal enthusiasm for the product – as was most certainly the case in Holland, home to the ebullient Ben Pon, and, conceivably due to a lack of other realistic options, a near certainty in Switzerland – dribbled into four countries, Belgium and Sweden being the other two. Contracts with operations in Luxembourg, Denmark, and Norway were next. The numbers involved were trivial, but then so was total Beetle production. However, by 1950 and only months into the life of the Export model and a coordinated strategy, a third of the total number of Beetles produced that year were driven out of Wolfsburg and out of Germany, destined for the 18 countries that had signed up to become a part of the Volkswagen empire. By the time of the all-important millionth Beetle celebrations, 700 out of the total daily output of 1,280 Beetles were for the export market.

Right: Heinz Nordhoff depicted in a manner appropriate to Frank Novotny's PR campaign for Volkswagen, and particularly the Beetle.

The 1960s would see extensive use made in advertising of Volkswagen's export programme, with a series of sales brochures variously entitled 'Why is the Volkswagen a favourite in 136 countries? Because ...', and 'The Volkswagen is a favourite in 136 countries. Why?' From snippets such as 'If fate should take you and your Volkswagen to Ruanda or Burundi someday, you'll find a friend down there already – your VW service', and 'In Switzerland ... Volkswagen has been the leader for years, despite a highly competitive market with more than 100 different makes of cars', to the more boastful 'More than 145,000 Australians drive a Volkswagen today. They need a rugged car "Down Under"', and the all-conquering 'Pound for pound, dollar for dollar, the Volkswagen is the best value for money. Up to now, 1,300,000 Americans have bought Volkswagens', Volkswagen's power and associated wealth as an exporter and more was complete.

Beetling in Britain

In early 1950s Britain anti-German feeling ran particularly high, and a patriotic desire to buy British goods was overwhelmingly predominant. Coupled with the fact that for many years Britain had been known as the home of the small car, Nordhoff's chances of launching a successful Beetle invasion seemed remote. While his chosen course in most countries was increasingly to become one of establishing his own sales and customer services network – Volkswagen Canada Ltd (created in September 1952) being a prime example at the time when manoeuvres in Britain were being contemplated – such a course of action simply wouldn't have worked. Instead, Nordhoff awarded the franchise to a British company, albeit

Right: The occasion of the 500,000th Beetle leaving the Wolfsburg assembly line on 3 July 1953 was celebrated with a roulette-style lottery in which several lucky workers won brand new cars.

Far left: A particularly attractive example of the commercial artwork of Bernd Reuters. Note how the artist has extended the length of the car, accentuated its curves, exaggerated features like the size of the sunroof and the dimensions of the rear window, and reduced the scale of the occupants in relation to the vehicle, making it appear larger than in reality. This kind of approach was common practice among car manufacturers in the 1950s.

Left: Reuters' artwork accompanied by the latest fashion statements in or around 1956. A car suitable for the ladies?

Below: The Beetle could go much faster when a photo was adapted to show lines indicating speed!

one headed by the Volkswagen mogul and pioneer assembler in the Republic of Ireland, Stephen O'Flaherty.

Crazily, there was a strong demand for small cars of any kind at the time, as British manufacturers exported 70 per cent of their production, but sales of the Beetle, starting in July 1953 with a batch of 200 oval-window cars, were somewhat disappointing at no more than 945 vehicles by the end of December – particularly so for Volkswagen Motors Ltd, which made a loss of a little over £4,000. When during the following year three out of every four cars landed at Harwich docks suffered some sort of politically motivated vandalism before they were moved on to the dealers, and Wolfsburg announced that due to demand elsewhere it was unable to produce any further right-hand-drive Beetles for the foreseeable future, the prospects appeared particularly disheartening. However, a personal appeal to Nordhoff by Volkswagen Motors Ltd's managing director, J.J. Graydon, resulted in a Saturday shift specifically to meet the demand for right-hand-drive cars, and slowly but surely matters improved. 3,260 Beetles were sold in Britain in 1954, while by 1958 that figure had reached a respectable 7,436. In 1959,

the 50,000th Beetle to be imported was presented to the widow of Colonel Charles Radclyffe. While the start had been slow and the numbers involved were still small

in comparison to what had been achieved in many other countries, every contribution to Volkswagen's ever-increasing profitability was worthwhile.

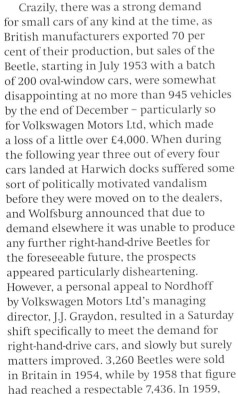

Above: 1953: in the background completed bodies await a matching chassis, while the cars in the foreground seem to lack little more than a fold-back canvas sunroof in some instances.

little short of 92,000 vehicles annually, with half-million celebrations taking place on 4 July 1967. Crucially, the Beetle had captured the Brazilian market as its best-selling car as early as 1962.

The American dream

Nordhoff's background with Opel helped him more than most to appreciate the crucial need to capture a percentage of the vast, cash-rich American market. Early attempts failed dismally. First to go was Beetle devotee and Dutch importer Ben Pon. Arriving in New York on 17 January 1949, he was met with a barrage of adverse publicity (the Beetle being roundly condemned as 'Hitler's car'), and a stonewall lack of interest amongst dealers who saw the vehicle as both tiny and grossly underpowered. Three weeks later, with his available funds exhausted, he sold the Beetle he had with him to pay his hotel bill. Nordhoff visited the United States himself in April of the same year and later reported the expedition to have been an 'utter failure'. The car that was presented to New York's Museum of Science and Industry as part of an exhibition of German products was subsequently sold, and together with Pon's Beetle accounted for the oft-quoted sum total of two sales made in the US during 1949.

Nordhoff's next act was an unusual one for him. He had become acquainted with Austrian Max Hoffmann, whose showroom of European cars had opened in Manhattan in 1947. In 1950 the first batch of 20 Beetles arrived at the premises of America's official East Coast VW Importer. Amidst the razzamatazz of a fully-fledged PR launch, and surrounded by such exotica as a bevy of Jaguars and even a pack of Porsches, Hoffman announced that it was his intention to import a minimum of 1,000 Beetles per month soon and no less than 3,000 cars every 30 days later. However, the reality behind the hype of such extravagant boasts never materialised. Hoffmann's emporium of costly metal for the wealthy was the wrong venue for the Beetle and neither he nor, more importantly, his salesmen believed in the product. The grand total of 157 cars sold in 1950 should have said it all to Nordhoff, but he chose to persevere.

Assembly and manufacture overseas

From a tacit interest aroused in early 1949 by José Thompson, head of Brasmotor, then the Chrysler importer for Brazil, to a visit by Nordhoff and the involvement of Chrysler's president C.T. Tomaz, Beetle sales became a reality in Brazil with effect from 23 March 1953. However, unlike many other operations, VW do Brasil was a member of an elite band, assembling rather than simply importing Beetles from the start. Brazil wasn't the first country to do this, it was merely the company that would become the most significant satellite of all as the decades unfolded.

CKD ('completely knocked down') kits, consisting of body panels, chassis components, and mechanical parts, most important of which was a ready-built engine, arrived in crates from Wolfsburg. Once unloaded they were assembled using varying amounts of locally sourced products, but most notably batteries, electrical components and wiring, glass and paint (leading to the emergence of shades local to a country with CKD facilities),

upholstery, and tyres. Before Brazil, CKD kits had been delivered to both the Republic of Ireland from 1950 and to SAMAD (South African Motor Assemblers and Distributors) from 1951, whose main business at the time was assembly of Austins and particularly Studebakers. Australia and Mexico both joined the assembly business in 1954, and others would follow suit later.

Between 1953 and 1957 a total of 2,268 Beetles were assembled in rented industrial premises in Ipiranga, a suburb of São Paulo, but in that latter year government permission was granted to build a full manufacturing plant, thus helping the Brazilian economy by reducing imports. The 107,600sq ft factory, headed by Nordhoff appointee Dr F.W. Schultz-Wenk, a German who would later take Brazilian citizenship, produced its first fully manufactured Beetle on 3 January 1959, a car boasting in excess of 95 per cent local content. During that year, 8,383 Beetles were built, a figure which more than doubled in 1960 and by the end of the Nordhoff era had soared to

Left: The sunroof Beetle always proved a popular alternative to the straightforward De Luxe saloon. With the camera in a semi-elevated position the scale of the sunroof opening is nicely depicted.

Below: The Volkswagen factory with the power station in the foreground pictured from the banks of the arterial Mittellandkanal in the 1950s.

Subsequent dismal performance in the form of a minuscule 390 sales in 1951 and a similarly depressing 601 the following year were at long last sufficient to galvanise Nordhoff into action in 1953. He despatched his export manager, Manuel Hinke, to the USA with the brief of retracting the 'franchise' by the end of the year if progress didn't meet Volkswagen's forecast. Hoffman in turn announced that he believed the Beetle to be an unsaleable commodity in the USA, no doubt feeling vindicated in his remarks when 1953 sales totalled no more than a paltry 1,013 cars. Nordhoff, at his autocratically most dynamic, ordered Hinke to use German personnel, already successful within the Volkswagen organisation, to resolve the issue, and within a short space of time Gottfried Lange from the Export Department was camped out in San Francisco, while maverick Will Van de Kamp, one-time Messerschmitt pilot and field salesman, arrived in New York unable to speak a word of English. The latter was the

Below: Although of no historical significance or new model pertinence, this delightful image illustrates more than many how the Beetle rapidly encompassed the world.

definitive persuasive salesman, the former the ultimate organiser and administrator.

For once, Nordhoff hadn't done Volkswagen the service he was normally so eminently capable of, but his 11th-hour resolve paid off. In 1954, 6,344 Beetles

were sold, the following year 30,928, and in 1956 the total jumped once more to 55,690. By 1959 – when, as will be seen, a future director general of Volkswagen took over – sales had increased to 150,601, and there was still much more to come.

A new engine

Although the Beetle couldn't really be regarded as underpowered when compared to its contemporaries of the early 1950s, to give it something of an edge over its rivals – particularly in the field of export markets – Nordhoff decreed that the wartime 25PS unit should be dispensed with in favour of something with a little more in the way of performance reserves. The answer came as an early Christmas present from Wolfsburg, when on 21 December 1953 the engine grew in cubic capacity from 1,131cc to 1,192cc and in output from a maximum of 25PS at 3,300rpm to what at the time was a significantly improved

30PS at 3,400rpm, or a potential 20 per cent gain in power. That the four inlet valves were increased in diameter from 28.6mm to 30mm to improve breathing, while generally the efficiency of the Solex carburettor had improved in recent times, also helped to emphasise the new engine's capabilities when compared directly with the old 25PS unit. Similarly, the boost in compression ratio from 5.8:1 to 6.1:1 assisted, although from the following August in a further refinement it increased once more to 6.6:1.

These specification revisions allowed cars fitted with the new 30PS engine to cruise at speeds of between 5 and 10mph faster, at least according to countless drivers who had experience of the 25PS unit's abilities. For once, though, Volkswagen's 68mph top-speed figure for its engine didn't appear particularly conservative as far as journalists were concerned. *The Autocar*, for example, achieved only 62.5mph in its road tests, while the best it could shave off the 0–50mph time was 0.7 of a second. *Motor*, on the other hand, was suitably impressed with its recorded top speed of 66.1mph, noting a 3mph improvement over that of the older 25PS unit. Better still, thanks to an undoubted increase in torque, they recorded an impressive five-second reduction in the time required to accelerate from 30 to 50mph in top gear.

One claim made of the 30PS engine certainly proved incredibly accurate. Volkswagen told potential buyers that not only was it likely to return in the region of 38mpg, but also that it was unlikely to require any major work within the first 75,000 miles of its existence. Numerous instances of 30PS engines with more than 200,000 miles on the clock are recorded, making it one of the most reliable power units ever to be produced by Wolfsburg.

Far left: The outgoing and amazingly exuberant Dutchman Ben Pon (left) was one of the first people to become involved in the Beetle's export story. Sadly, his attempt to conquer the American market on Nordhoff's behalf ended in failure.

Left: Nordhoff's own trip to the USA in search of Beetle sales ended without success, but that didn't stop the director general making expeditions to many other countries in his campaign to make the Beetle a worldwide phenomenon.

Left: The majority of the Beetles leaving Wolfsburg's giant conveyer belt in this picture were awaiting export to America, as evidenced by the two-tier bumpers and the bullet-shaped indicators alongside each car's headlamps.

In the last days of 1953, Volkswagen upgraded their 25PS engine to 30PS. Visually very similar to its predecessor, the new power unit was noticeably more powerful and certainly as good if not better than many of the Beetle's contemporaries.

The fully detailed Wolfsburg Crest boot lid badge was a part of the De Luxe model Beetle's specification from April 1951 to October 1962, although its design was modified/ simplified in August 1959 for the '60 model year.

The dashboards of cars built after October 1952 and before August 1957 were of the style featured in the image. More attractive than those of earlier cars, the principal drawbacks were a rather small glove-box compartment and a lack of symmetrical design. The large grille in the middle of the dashboard concealed the radio speaker where it was fitted.

Comparing this image of an early De Luxe oval-window Beetle with that of the earlier split-window model on page 53, the cars appear remarkably similar. Such a notion was always at the heart of the Beetle's evolution. Nordhoff refused to be at the beck and call of the men he referred to as 'hysterical stylists'.

The bud vase pictured was a popular accessory in the 1950s and could be purchased in a variety of guises. So iconic was it in nature that when Volkswagen launched the New Beetle in the late 1990s, the bud vase was part of the package. The clock in the grille was also an accessory available for this style of dashboard, but was much less common.

In Beetle enthusiast terminology the image depicts a heart-shaped tail light, so called due to the appearance of the stop lens on the top of the lamp. Introduced in October 1952, such lights were discontinued on all cars by August 1955. Although attractive, the design was hardly very practical!

The simple act of removing the metal between the two panes of glass forming the Beetle's rear window modernised the look of the car and increased the glass size by 23 per cent. The deed, which took place on 10 March 1953, led to the new cars being given the highly unofficial name of 'Ovals', or 'Oval-window Beetles'.

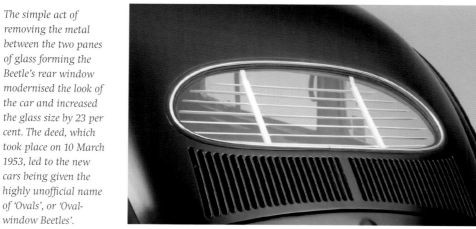

It was during the era of the Oval that Beetle sales really gathered pace, spurred on by the American market's acceptance of the concept at long last. Soon to become a cult car, this simple full-frontal shot does little to reveal the charisma of the car. The badge bar is a period accessory fitted by an enthusiastic owner.

Sales-enhancing improvements

Although the creation of the oval-shaped window appeared to act as a catalyst in demand both at home and abroad, Nordhoff gave no thought to stopping there. Accordingly, seemingly trivial amendments continued to be the meat of many a specification guide. One change to previous patterns began to emerge as, in recognition of the potential importance of the American market, variations emerged between Beetles produced for domestic or European consumption and those destined to travel on the highways of the USA and, to a lesser extent, Canada. Notable examples included the October 1954 introduction of a new style of rear-light case which had the effect of making the brake lights more easily visible, a feature which didn't filter through to other cars for a further ten months. Sealed-beam headlamps, easily distinguishable by clear outer lenses, became the norm for US-bound cars in April 1955 and the following month all such Beetles benefited from indicators rather than semaphores, something that wouldn't occur in Europe for a further few years, and at a time when the US model had already undergone a further upgrade. The new front indicators thus became something of a novelty in later years, being mounted as they were close to the outer edges of the US Beetle's headlamps and taking the shape of a bullet.

The final diversification of this period was brought about by the variance in the relative height of the Beetle's bumpers to those of the average Detroit-manufactured saloon, an inconsistency which inevitably led to parking nudges and scrapes to the detriment of the car's appearance. Wolfsburg's response to US dealer and customer complaints was to increase the size, or rather the height, of the Beetle's over-riders on both its front and rear bumpers to support an additional cylinder-shaped bar to sit above the original curved blade. Support braces attached to the bodyshell afforded sufficient rigidity for the new arrangement, while at the US specification car's rear the additional rail wasn't continuous in nature, thus allowing the engine lid to be opened

without the need to revise its design. To say that the new bumpers (soon to be nicknamed 'towel-rail bumpers') were attractive is an understatement, and although they never became a standard part of the specification of European-market cars, they could soon be requested as an accessory item.

Coinciding with the arrival of the millionth such car the Beetle was given a general facelift, and although it affected neither the size nor shape of its windows, and didn't involve any form of engine upgrade, it was easy to distinguish the latest Beetle from its earlier counterparts.

That the changes occurred at the beginning of August 1955 was also significant, for up until this point Volkswagen had tended to follow a haphazard arrangement of launching any revision as and when it was ready. Think,

for example, of the De Luxe Beetle's launch in July 1949, the upgraded edition of October 1952 vintage, and more recently the oval rear window of March 1953 and the 30PS engine of December the same year. US practice, however, was wherever possible to launch a series of changes all at the same time and, with effect from August 1955, Wolfsburg followed suit. From this point onwards cars produced in the eighth calendar month and onwards of a given year adopted the title of the next. Hence cars built in August 1955 were referred to as '56 models.

The '56 model year Beetle featured a revised exhaust system with twin tailpipes and, as it sat some 18mm higher within the framework of the vehicle, involved a redesign of the rear valance to include two cut-outs to accommodate the chromed tailpipes. Fitted to cars destined for the

Left: One of several well-known images designed to illustrate the Beetle's popularity across the world.

This page: The assembly line as caught on camera in 1956. Daily output of Beetles had risen from 312 in 1950 to more than 1,000 by the time this series of pictures was taken. By the end of the decade production would have tripled, but there were still waiting lists for Beetles.

USA from May 1955, European models now also benefited from the revised style of rear-light cluster, although the function was dual rather than triple as semaphores continued to serve as the means of indicating a change in direction. In all cases the taillight pods were moved some 60mm further up the wings, the argument being one of increased visibility. Moving to the interior, the quarter-light catches were improved to make it more difficult for the light-fingered to gain entry to the car. So that the single gauge could be read more easily by the driver, the design of the steering wheel was altered with its two spokes being positioned off-centre. The tunnel-mounted heater knob was moved further forwards to make access easier, while the gear lever became cranked in design for similar reasons. The front seats became larger and consequently more comfortable, while not only were the backrests now adjustable to three positions, but the runner rails were altered to accommodate seven rather than two positions. With the back seat also becoming larger, Volkswagen's objective was evident – to make it easier for all shapes and sizes of drivers and passengers to enjoy their journeys. Finally, apart from a host of other more minor specification changes, the petrol tank was changed in shape allowing owners to store 85 litres of luggage in the front boot, rather than the previous 70 litres.

This more detailed than usual analysis of the changes made to the Beetle for one particular model year hopefully illustrates that while every now and then a more drastic redesign would occur, Nordhoff was true to his word and ensured that every possible attempt was made to make the Beetle ever more saleable to Volkswagen's customers. The policy undoubtedly not only paid off at the time, but enhanced Volkswagen's status as a producer of particularly well thought out and superbly executed vehicles for many years to come.

Beetle benevolence

With the rapid escalation in production numbers experienced as the 1950s began to gather pace, the manufacturing costs for each Beetle inevitably began to fall. The decidedly non-greedy Nordhoff offered a wonderful dose of royal icing on the cake of the one-millionth celebrations by reducing the retail price of all Beetles. The base or Standard model dropped from 3,950DM to 3,790DM, the much more popular De Luxe from 4,850DM to 4,700DM, and the hand-crafted, out-sourced Cabriolet from 6,500DM to 5,990DM.

Hand in hand with this gesture the Beetle workforce were granted full pay during periods of illness, while earlier Nordhoff had instigated a profit-sharing scheme, had used Volkswagen's own building firm to construct additional modern housing at a time when government funds were unavailable, and even bestowed on Wolfsburg a swimming pool costing in excess 1,000,000DM. The Beetle's success story made Nordhoff the great patron and father of his people.

Celebrating the millionth Beetle

Novotny and his team spent a frantic eight months preparing an appropriately lavish event spanning both a Friday and Saturday to celebrate and at the same time publicise Volkswagen's achievement in producing its millionth Beetle. Wolfsburg's entire workforce and the all-encompassing family that made up the population of its burgeoning city, distributors and dealers not just from Germany but from each and every nation where the Beetle's roots were now established, and well over 1,000 national and international motoring correspondents and journalists, had been invited. A total approaching 160,000 people were present, all with one purpose in mind – they were to witness the anointing of the millionth Beetle by the man who had made it possible, Heinz Nordhoff.

Specially produced souvenir programmes carefully itemised the festival's progress while also serving as a timely reminder to any slumbering journalists of the Beetle's influence across the world. The message behind the pageantry of dancers from the Moulin Rouge in Paris, the significance of the spirituals sung by South African choirs, the essence of the musical ceilidh provided by Scottish dancers performing to the accompaniment of bagpipes, the exciting modern brilliance of the Camino Band from South America and its accompanying bevy of scantily clad girls, the frantic whirl of riotous colour offered by troops of Swiss nationals as they waved the flags of nations – none of this was lost on the subconscious of the gathered crowds; each and every parade represented a country where the Beetle now stood firm. Timely words of congratulation from pioneers in Beetle export and import, from initiating assemblers, and remarkably adept managers, each reinforced by carefully crafted messages posted in the Festival programme, hammered home the story too. The Beetle's home was no longer just in Germany: in each of five continents its residence had mushroomed: 23 locations were listed for Europe, from Andorra to Trieste; 33 in North and Latin America, from Argentina to Venezuela; 26 in Africa, from Algeria to Uganda; 7 in Australasia, from Australia to Tahiti; and 19 in Asia, from Aden to Turkey.

Nordhoff's appearances were as usual polished and professional. His first act was to attach the magical chassis plate to the 1,000,000th car, a far from standard Beetle. The choice of finish was skilful, for not only did the rich hues of gold glisten in the concentration of arc-lamps designed for the multitude of press and cinema cameras, but also its diamanté-encrusted trim package, which extended beyond the bumpers and headlamp rims to the running board strips, waistline and

This page: Celebrations of unprecedented extravagance heralded the arrival of the millionth Beetle on 6 August 1955. Volkswagen played host to its own workers, representatives from its sales force across the world, and a myriad of journalists. Nordhoff not only made speeches but also received both the Order of Merit of the Federal Republic of Germany and the Freedom of the town of Wolfsburg.

Far left: The millionth Beetle has been preserved for posterity and is resident in Wolfsburg's Autostadt. Finished in gold metallic paint, its bumpers are diamanté encrusted while its headlining is a somewhat garish pink.

Left: Guests invited to celebrate production of the millionth Beetle on 6 August 1955 were presented with a souvenir programme.

boot lid brightwork, sparkled, dazzled, and twinkled as the cameras flashed. The simple act of opening either the driver or passenger door revealed a galaxy of pink-patterned flock still further guaranteed to set it apart from the relatively austere cars produced across the motoring world, and certainly not just restricted to Volkswagen.

Nordhoff's speech to the press was wide ranging. Driving home the point that the millionth Beetle and its contemporaries were truly international vehicles, the director general confirmed that of the cars produced each year on average 55 per cent were now destined for export. In 1955, 35,000 would go to the USA, 28,000 to Sweden, 18,000 to Belgium, 14,000 to Holland, 12,000 to Switzerland and 10,000 to Austria. Even so, the Volkswagen Company he had created was hungry for more. 'We are far from sitting on the top of the world', Nordhoff told his audience, whilst implying that it was the responsibility of everyone present to take home what they had seen and deliver the Beetle package as many times as it was necessary for an audience to succumb to its charms.

However, it was Nordhoff's final appearance at the spectacular that set Volkswagen and the Beetle apart from the rest. To a magnificent fanfare provided by the combined might of 12 orchestras, the director general mounted the 15m high podium, acknowledged the tumultuous applause and voiced thanks to the workforce for the unprecedented achievement they had brought about. 'These celebrations', he proclaimed, 'have provided a glimpse of the world which Volkswagen has conquered and will continue to conquer.' No novelist, no playwright, no dramatist could have engineered a more skilfully polished or appropriate performance – Nordhoff and the Beetle had assumed the status of deities.

Left: Flanked by two 1938 Beetles (a cabriolet and a saloon) to its right, and 1965 and 1976 models to its left, the millionth Beetle stands in front of the oldest and most widely recognised part of the factory.

1957–1967 CLASSIC BEETLES

The 1958 model year Beetle, launched in August 1957, might be regarded as exhibiting the single biggest leap forward of any since the era of the VW38 prototypes. The characteristics the latest model demonstrated would endure too. The brand new style of dashboard would still be more or less current 45 years later when Beetle production finally ground to a halt, while the introduction of a rear window almost twice as large as that of the '57 model year, although subject to further if not so generous enlargements, again cast in metal the look the car would present for the ensuing decades.

However, the 1960s Beetles were to be equally significant in their own way, aesthetics on this occasion playing second fiddle to progress in power and other mechanical advances. 1961 models saw the first engine upgrade for over six years. August 1965 would see a bigger brother for the once staple 1200 models, a car with 40PS at its disposal, while within the space of just 12 short months it too was eclipsed by the vehicle that deserved its accolade of the 'hot Beetle', the 1,493cc 1500 Beetle, a driver's car with 44PS at its disposal and for most markets disc brakes at its front. Suddenly, the addition of synchromesh on first gear in the summer of 1960 paled into insignificance.

Left: Followng the upgrade in rear window size in August 1957, Beetles entered a classic era of graceful aesthetics. Dating such cars to a given year isn't easy but if it is Euro specification models and has indicator housings on the front wings, the car has to be of '60 vintage or later.

Main picture and right: Transformed! That is the best way to describe the Beetles that rolled off the Wolfsburg assembly line in August 1957 at the start of the '58 model year. The size of the rear window had been increased by 95 per cent and suddenly the Beetle looked almost modern! One consequence of this change was that the number of air intake slots below the glass were increased but dramatically reduced in size. This car features the rare anodised aluminium air intake trims.

Right: Steering wheel design changed with monotonous regularity, although all De Luxe models were finished in ivory plastic until the summer of August 1965. The style depicted was first introduced in August 1955 and was replaced four years later at the end of July 1959.

Left: As noteworthy as the increase in glass size was the all-new dashboard, the design of which would remain more or less unchanged until the end of Beetle production over 45 years later, (the exception being the curved screen, plastic dash 1303 models). Undoubtedly the most aesthetically balanced of dashboard designs, the glove-box was larger than it had been previously, while the single dial was now firmly lodged in front of the driver. Instruments on De Luxe models were finished in ivory coloured plastic, as was the steering wheel. The decorative chrome strip would survive as part of the design for more than a decade.

The ever-faithful 30PS engine, reliable and well known for its longevity if suitably looked after. Although replaced on De Luxe models in the summer of 1960 by a 34PS power unit, the smaller engine remained the mainstay of the base model, the Standard, for a further few years.

Popular vinyl was selected to trim most Beetles, although some markets were favoured with cloth seat upholstery as an option. Without question, cars assembled in the later years of the 1950s and the first three or four years of the next decade were the most pleasing to the aesthetics' eye. Note too the quality of the fittings; chrome, two tone door cards and more.

Just as the size of the rear window had been increased so too had that of the windscreen of the '58 model year car, although in percentage terms the change in this instance was far less dramatic. However, while only amounting to a 17 per cent enlargement, as the glass had nibbled its way into the Beetle's roof, the car looked less antiquated and more airy.

Right: De Luxe Beetles offered before August 1961 lacked a fuel gauge, relying instead on a tap, which when the car began to splutter could be flicked allowing a reserve gallon of petrol to be drawn upon. Many owners weren't happy with such an arrangement and fitted auxiliary equipment such as this gauge supplied by the manufacturer Dehne.

Left: From the heart-shaped tail lights of the car featured on pages 78 to 81, in August 1955, earlier in the USA, Beetles acquired the style of rear lights pictured, a design that would remain in place beyond the turn of the decade. Dual purpose in nature, the lamps lit when the brake pedal was selected, and at night when the Beetle's sidelights or headlamps were switched on. From August 1960 and the introduction of wing mounted indicators at the front of the car, the case also carried a flashing function!

Left: The Beetle's carrying capacity was restricted in part by the intrusion of the petrol tank, although modifications which took effect in August 1955 improved the situation somewhat. The real change wouldn't come until the 1961 model year when, with a new shape, the tank was concealed below the boot lining. The spare wheel tool kit is a highly sought-after accessory.

The big-window Beetle

With yet another substantial increase in sales and corresponding production in 1957, the latter being up by 14 per cent worldwide, and the former by 13 per cent in West Germany alone, a waiting list for cars of many weeks' duration, and a car that, as the time taken to build it became less and less, was actually cheaper to buy than it ever had been before, there was no apparent need for an updated Beetle. However, such a move or lack of it was unthinkable for Nordhoff's Volkswagen; the Beetle was destined to keep ahead of its rivals for many years to come.

Without a doubt, the most striking external feature of the 1958 model year Beetle was its rear screen and a large glass area that cut into every direction of its surrounding metalwork, bringing about a 95 per cent increase in the total size of the rear window, in an instant not only making the car more modern in its appearance but also creating a much safer vehicle to drive thanks to the vast increase in rearward visibility and an enormous reduction in blind-spots. Although it was both impossible and unnecessary to attempt a similar increase in the size of the Beetle's windscreen, the car's roof panel was planed back a bit and the 'A' pillars sufficiently sanded down to balance the vehicle's appearance with a 17 per cent increase in glass size at the front.

Inevitably, other areas had to be modified to accommodate such startling changes and most notably these consisted of engine cooling vents below the rear window, which, although increased in number from two banks of 21 each to a single run of 50, were now considerably smaller. Although not necessary in terms of a requirement for a reduction in size, the engine lid was redesigned to balance with the look of the window, more or less losing its once sacred 'W' shape, but in the process gaining a larger hood in which to conceal the number plate light and, more importantly, a slightly closer to vertical and usefully higher from the ground location on which to mount the car's registration number.

As this isn't a specification guide, only passing reference needs be made to the decision to abandon the bullet-shaped front indicators exclusive to the US market in favour of the first of a series of elongated teardrop-shaped housings for this purpose, and only then to bemoan the seemingly antiquated reliance on semaphore indictors for all European-market cars. Why Volkswagen chose to cling on to such archaic devices when other manufacturers were moving away from them in droves, will remain a matter of mystery, other than to say neither quality nor cost had anything to do with the decision. On such a note, one oddity that did disappear was

Right: With the advent of a much larger rear window promotional material suddenly included numerous shots of the Beetle from the rear.

Below: The new dashboard of '58 model year vintage was beautifully illustrated in sales brochures of that era.

reliance on a most unusual roller-style accelerator, which was relegated to Volkswagen's museum in favour of a more seemingly conventional oblong-shaped, rubber-covered treadle.

Of equal significance to the Beetle's new rear window was the introduction of a completely redesigned dashboard, only the second such change since the arrival of the VW38 prototypes and, perhaps more unusually, destined to be the company's last. Unquestionably the most balanced in terms of design, the new unit retained the helpful position of the car's sole gauge directly in front of the steering wheel and balanced its appearance with two carefully carved grilles, the larger of the two designed to conceal a speaker for the radio, replicating the shape of the new and much larger glove-box which was situated directly in front of the passenger. The central section was allocated to switches and knobs for a combination of headlamps, wipers, and choke, all conveniently located around a period petite blanking panel ready to receive a radio. At a time when the majority of men smoked and the habit was becoming increasingly prevalent amongst women, the ashtray's location above the centre tunnel and within the base section of the dashboard was decidedly convenient. With the careful attention to detail for which Volkswagen was renowned, the package was rounded off by the inclusion of a horizontal shiny trim strip, while the use of attractive ivory-coloured pulls and switches was maintained.

Undoubtedly sales would have increased with or without such changes, but nevertheless a vindicatory increase in production numbers amounting to nearly 19 per cent was experienced in the restyled Beetle's first full year of production. Volkswagen had become unstoppable, and just when it seemed that Dame Fortune couldn't possibly have any more delights hidden up her voluminous sleeve to assist Nordhoff another one presented itself, this time round in the form of a ground-breaking answer to a potential threat.

Right: Another marketing image, this time indicating the Beetle's capabilities in snowy conditions.

Promoting the Beetle – Doyle Dane Bernbach

As suggested in the previous chapter, Beetle sales in the United States had been steadily rising through the later years of the 1950s, although the ad hoc methods through which this had been achieved were a cause of constant concern to Nordhoff. Following the departure of the controversial Will Van de Kamp, Nordhoff turned his thoughts to Carl Hahn, a young economist who had so impressed the director general several years earlier that he had been taken into the inner sanctum at Wolfsburg before being assigned to the export department's sales promotion operation.

Nordhoff told author Walter Henry Nelson that, despite Hahn's lack of belief in his own skills, he was convinced that he was the man: 'For decades, no one believed that European cars could ever be a success in the United States. Then, after the war, the British showed that it could be done. I knew that we could do the same ... I told Hahn I wanted VW to have more dealers in the USA, fresh dealers, and dealers who wanted to sell Volkswagens exclusively. We had not come to the US market to be fifth wheel to the Big Three ... I suggested to him that he go after people who had no automobile franchises at all, because so many of the best dealers had been taken on by Detroit.'

Hahn took his master's message to heart and when the Detroit giants of Ford, General Motors, and Chevrolet each announced launch dates during 1960 for the compact cars they had been planning, he had already taken fitting action in a way appropriate to the American market to which he had fast become adapted. Hahn decided to break an unwritten rule that sales alone were sufficient to sell the Beetle's undoubted merits, and to advertise. In so doing, perhaps unknowingly at the time, he created the foundation stones for the car gaining a cult status that none before, and few if any since, have achieved.

Hahn's choice of advertising agency was superb, for not only did it work in

un charme !

Left: A clever publicity shot illustrating not only the Beetle's performance capabilities, but also its ability to operate effectively in dry, dusty, desert conditions.

America but, as word spread like lightning, it also elevated Nordhoff's beloved automobile to hitherto unimaginable heights, with whole new strata of society becoming immersed in its aura as the 'must-have' car.

The introduction of the Chevrolet Corvair, the Ford Falcon, and General Motors' Valiant had indeed the anticipated disastrous effect on virtually all European imports. From a high in 1960 sales figures were slashed in half, falling to 378,622 in 1961 and still further in 1962 to 339,160. Only the Beetle survived unscathed, despite Chevrolet's general manager's prediction of 1959 that 'Volkswagen would be out of business in this country in two years'.

While a bevy of advertising agencies were eager to acquire Volkswagen's work, few if any presented anything of

great value to Hahn as the rounds of endless presentations ensued. Advertising generally was dull, relied heavily on text-heavy material, and while a generation later we might be awestruck by some of the artwork produced by a series of commercial artists, aimed at creating sleek, elongated, speed-implying vehicles from the most basic of cars, the Beetle included, there was nothing new to inspire Hahn. At best this kind of advertising was false, at worst it was blatantly dishonest. Fortunately for Hahn, Arthur Stanton, a Volkswagen distributor in New York, and chairman of an independent group determined not to be outdone by Detroit, had the answer. He had charged an agency with just ten years' credit rating to its name with the task of promoting a new service centre he had developed, and had been suitably delighted with the result.

Bill Bernbach and Ned Doyle had previously worked for Grey Advertising, an old school agency, but in 1949 they had teamed up with Mac Dane, who had a small agency of his own, and together they formed Doyle Dane Bernbach, or DDB. Although they had already done work for big names like El Al and the New York retailer Ohrbach's it was through their alliance with Volkswagen that they hit the big time. Their strategy when they met Volkswagen was one of honesty, and not only did such an approach appeal to Hahn, it was also what he wanted for the Beetle.

When Hahn spoke of people having to wait for six months to buy a Beetle, Bernbach responded with the first draft headline, 'Why do people wait six months for a VW when they can get any other car immediately?' This was subsequently revised, taking out the direct references both to other manufacturers and a specific waiting time, leaving in place the honest one-message question, 'Why are people buying Volkswagens faster than they can be made?'

Hahn was insistent and DDB were eager to see Beetles being assembled at Wolfsburg before the campaign gathered momentum. Walter Henry Nelson, author of *Small Wonder*, was fortunate enough to gain an interview with Bill Bernbach and to discover why the DDB campaign of honesty emerged in the way it did:

'A whole team of us went over there. We spent days talking to engineers, production men, executives, workers on the assembly line. We marched side by side with the molten metal that hardened into the engine, and kept going until every part was finally in its place. We watched finally as a man climbed behind the steering wheel, pumped the first life into the newborn bug and drove it off the line. We were immersed in the making of a Volkswagen and knew what our theme had to be. We knew what distinguished this car. We knew what we had to tell the American public ... We had seen the quality of materials used. We had seen the almost incredible precautions taken to avoid mistakes. We had seen the costly system of inspection that turned back cars that would never have been turned

down by the consumer. We had seen the impressive efficiency that resulted in such an unbelievably low price for such a quality product. We had seen the pride of craftsmanship in the worker that made him exceed even the high standards set for him. Yes, this was an honest car. We had found our selling proposition.'

DDB's interpretation of honesty – an all embracing no-nonsense single photograph untouched in the studio; a one-message pithy strap-line designed to reinforce the image; and three carefully clipped columns of succinct text to reinforce

both – took not only the advertising world by storm, but the American nation too. By 1961/2 they were confident enough to run an ad that lacked any form of picture, leaving a blank space where it would normally have been. The emptiness coupled to the strap-line said it all: 'We don't have anything to show you in our new models', confirmed the perfection of the Beetle's established design. 'After we paint the car we paint the paint'; 'Repair 'em? I've got enough parts to build them!'; 'The only water a Volkswagen needs is the water you wash it with'; 'Our number

Above and opposite: The construction of the 13-storey administration building in 1959, which dwarfed the height of the adjoining factory, illustrated the pace of Volkswagen's expansion – certainly a message of continually outgrowing existing facilities and production targets. The aerial shot commands a dramatically imposing view of the factory's 1.5km frontage.

one salesman' (against a picture of a mechanic at work under a Beetle); 'Lemon', with an accompanying text that started 'This Volkswagen missed the boat. The chrome strip on the glove compartment is blemished and must be replaced...'. The list of classics was seemingly endless.

The famous Italian designer suggested one change.

Just because the appearance of the Volkswagen doesn't change from year to year, don't think we take it for granted.

Some time ago, we called in a world-famous Italian body designer and we asked him what changes he would recommend in the design of the Volkswagen.

He studied it and studied it. Then he said, "Make the rear window larger."

"That's all?"

"That's all."

We did, starting with the '58 VW. The Volkswagen is never changed to make it different. Only to make it better.

Changes take place throughout the year. 19 functional improvements have been made in the 1960 VW so far, improvements in handling, in ride, in durability. But your eye wouldn't detect these changes unless we pointed them out. A nice Volkswagen touch is that most of the new parts are interchangeable; they can also be used on previous-year VWs.

We think the Volkswagen approach to automobile design makes sense. It might even turn out to be the most advanced styling idea of all.

The only water a Volkswagen needs is the water you wash it with.

All car engines must be cooled. But how? Conventional cars are cooled by water. The Volkswagen engine is cooled by air.

The advantages are astonishing, when you think about it. Your Volkswagen cannot boil over in summer or freeze in winter, since air neither boils nor freezes.

You need no anti-freeze. You have no radiator problems. In fact, you have no radiator.

In midsummer traffic jams, your VW can idle indefinitely, while other cars and tempers boil.

The doughty Volkswagen engine is unique in still other ways. Its location in the rear means better traction (in mud, sand, ice, snow, where other cars skid, you go). And since it is cast of aluminum-magnesium alloys, you save weight and increase efficiency. Your VW delivers an honest 32 miles to the gallon, regular driving, regular gas.

You will probably never need oil between changes.

A car for the rich and famous

So much did the Beetle become a must-have symbol of the 1960s that stars of the day were more than happy to endorse the product. Imagine, then, calling in on a US dealership and thumbing through their latest Beetle brochure entitled 'Why do so many people buy Volkswagens?' and alighting on the headline, 'I started buying them when I started as an actor. Today, I drive them out of loyalty.' Those were the words of Paul Newman. At the time he had owned four Beetles. The accompanying DDB script was smoothly skilful as two short extracts demonstrate.

Owning four Beetles, the copywriter claimed, made Paul Newman 'a typical VW owner. Because when it's time for the typical VW owner to buy a new car, he usually buys another new VW. Why such

loyalty? Maybe it's because people who started out liking the idea behind our car like the idea that we've remained loyal to the idea behind our car...'

'Over the years just about everything has changed. Except the way our car looks. Even the way people look at it has changed. In 1949, it brought a lot of laughs. By 1959, it had a lot of people you'd never think would own one, owning one. Of course, with the ready comment that "it's our second car." But today, there's nothing wrong with owning a VW. And just a VW. And Paul Newman probably proves that best with his VW: "It's *my* car. I drive it every place I go."'

Well-known Beetle-owning people of the 1960s included King Baudouin and Queen Fabiola of the Belgians, Princess

Margaret and the Earl of Snowdon, Charles Lindbergh (the American aviator, author, inventor, and explorer), Dr Benjamin Spock (famous for his book of baby and child care), and, perhaps inevitably, John Lennon, the famous two-legged Beatle.

Perhaps the ultimate Beetle accolade came in 1969 when Walt Disney Studios released the first of their 'Herbie' films, endearingly entitled *The Love Bug* and starring a white-sunroofed saloon with a whim to triumph against life's evils. Carrying the now legendary '53' decal on its boot lid and doors, plus a front to back stripe, the original Herbie subsequently spawned many copies, all of which were created out of a wish to be enveloped in and surrounded by the Beetle's charismatic magic.

Demand for even higher production levels

At the start of the 1960s Nordhoff still faced one seemingly insurmountable problem – Volkswagen's continuing inability to match supply to demand. Between the bumper output year of 1958 and 1959 Beetle production rose from 451,526 to 575,407 cars, or a further 27 per cent. The next 12 months saw demand increase by similar proportions, resulting in another year of substantial increases over the previous one at Wolfsburg, with the factory working to seam-bursting maximum capacity to produce the additional 164,036 cars it achieved. Whether Nordhoff would have acquiesced

with Carl Hahn's off-the-cuff remark that 'No one thought it possible to sell so many motor-cars' is debatable, as he had already planned that Volkswagen should build more and more Beetles.

Speaking in March 1960 Nordhoff revealed that the decision had been taken two years previously to plan decisive steps to 'normalise' the relationship between supply and demand. In 1959, investments totalled a little short of 500,000 million DM and resulted in an increase in daily production of 1,000 vehicles. The course of action for 1960 was virtually identical, with a similar amount being invested and, by the end of

the year, capacity once again increased to the tune of a further 1,000 Volkswagens daily. Nordhoff was right in his assumption that with such a level of investment he would 'finally' be able to 'deliver Volkswagens to customers without a waiting period'.

Below: The Beetle's status as a cult car took another leap forward when Disney created Herbie, the human car. Contrary to many rumours, the various cars that played the role of Herbie weren't remotely controlled or computer driven. Top stunt drivers operated them, making use of a steering wheel that was repositioned backwards. The bulkhead was replaced by a curtain so that a suitably enraged Herbie could swallow large objects via an open boot lid! Herbies varied considerably in specification – note the Europa bumpers on this example.

Right: Although outwardly little different from its immediate predecessors, the '61 model year Beetle included a number of improvements, most notable of which were the 34PS engine and all-synchromesh gearbox.

A new decade and a better Beetle

Right: The last brochure to feature the artwork of Bernd Reuters. The artist had been dead for several years by the time it was published, other artists having to add later attributes such as the wing-mounted indicators. Times were changing and Volkswagen would soon be reliant on cleverly posed photography.

The Beetle produced after Wolfsburg's summer holidays in August 1960, and hence a '61 model year car, carried a number of features that made it a better product than previous examples. Without delving too deeply into the specifics of every widget that was changed, buyers no longer had to contend with the prospect of double-declutching when engaging first gear, due to a new all-synchromesh four-speed gearbox which had a redesigned one-piece casing and revised, more useful ratios on third and fourth gears. Thanks to a redesigned petrol tank, luggage space in the front boot increased from a restrictive 85 litres to a more comfortable 140 litres. Undoubtedly as important to European owners who had long since tired of flapping their arms about as a back-up to the ineffective semaphore turn signals,

modern indicators, in the style of those bestowed on the US-specification Beetles three years earlier, adorned the front wings, although the single lens housing at the rear, which now incorporated the three separate functions of night lights, slowing down or stopping, as well as turning, lacked a little foresight and was destined to be redesigned within a 12-month period. Dirty windscreens were also a thing of the past, as all cars were fitted with screen-washer nozzles, a one-litre water bottle located behind the spare wheel, and a dash-mounted push-button pump.

While each of these modifications was sufficient to grab the headlines, at least in Volkswagen terms, one other change was of far greater significance: the 1961 Beetle came with a more powerful engine. From 30PS at 3,400rpm the 'new'

Left: Volkswagen's modern-day image of a 1961 model year Beetle on display in Wolfsburg's Stiftung museum heralds Nordhoff's vision for the Beetle in his second decade as director general: no change, just continual improvement.

engine developed a maximum of 34PS at 3,600rpm, a change that might have gone unnoticed elsewhere but at Volkswagen was as significant as anything attempted since Nordhoff's arrival over 12 years previously. Nor was Nordhoff going to spend unnecessary cash willy-nilly, for the 34PS unit was essentially a version of the engine developed a year earlier for the much larger and heavier Transporter, a genuinely underpowered vehicle by the end of the 1950s. Capacity remained the same at 1,192cc, as did the bore and stroke at 77mm x 64mm respectively; it was a number of detail changes and an increase in the compression ratio from 6.6:1 to 7.0:1 that brought about improved performance.

As usual, Volkswagen were at best conservative and at worst simply coy about the latest offering, merely suggesting a 4mph increase in the Beetle's top speed, from a previously recorded 68mph to a

Left: Cabriolet and sunroof models bask in the sunshine of an alpine holiday, circa 1961.

more useful 72mph. It was left to scrutiny of the small print to discern a meaningful three-second cut in the time it took to reach 50mph, which was now achieved in what one of the many motoring magazines described as a 'never-all-that-sluggish' 18 seconds.

A considerable number of modifications were at the heart of the new engine and these included a stronger crankcase, a more robust crankshaft, a modified fuel-pump drive, a removable dynamo pedestal, and wider spacing of the cylinder barrels. In an attempt to reduce the amount of noise the engine made, a smaller crankshaft pulley and a larger dynamo pulley enabled the cooling fan to run at a slower speed, while to the surprise of more than a few the new Solex carburettor (28 PICT) was fitted with a thermostatically controlled automatic choke.

Amazingly, the 34PS engine was still available as the Beetle entered another decade of production, and for the 1976 model year once again became the mainstay of the (albeit truncated) Beetle range. Indeed, for as long as Beetles were sold in Germany the 34PS engine was available, affording it a run of just over a quarter of a century.

Five million Beetles – ten million Beetles

As 1961 drew to a festive close Beetle production arrived at the milestone point of five million cars of a single type having been produced. Following manufacture of the two-millionth Beetle on 28 December 1957, the three-millionth on 25 August 1959, and the four-millionth on 9 November 1960, the attendant ceremonials weren't in the same league as those of a little over six years earlier, nor was the purpose behind bedecking the car with flowers quite the same. Nevertheless, Nordhoff took the opportunity to remind those attending of Volkswagen's achievements over such a relatively short space of time, and instead of saving the car for posterity by mothballing it in Volkswagen's museum he presented

Right: The five-millionth Beetle left the Wolfsburg assembly line on 5 December 1961.

it to the International Red Cross, to the accompaniment of a firework display of press cameras.

'We have good reason to be proud', he said, for the Beetle was 'a symbol of one of the biggest industrial successes ever reached … the result of hard, unremitting work and of diligent attention to a correctly set goal … [That goal can be defined as] developing one model of car to the height of its technical excellence; … dedicating ourselves to the attainment of the highest quality; … destroying the notion that such high-quality cars can only be attained at high prices; … giving the car the highest value and building it so that it retains that value.'

Volkswagen, the Beetle, and Nordhoff – the three formed one holy trinity – were

Above: In honour of the completion of the five-millionth Beetle the Bavarian State Mint issued both gold and silver coins bearing the car on one side and its greatest protagonist, Heinz Nordhoff, on the other.

Left: Although Nordhoff would see more production barriers fall in his remaining years as director general, the arrival, on 15 September 1964, of the ten-millionth Beetle to be produced since the war was certainly a significant occasion.

*Right: Antarctica 1 – a
superb publicity ploy.
The Australian National
Antarctic Research
Expedition took a
standard specification
Beetle to Antarctica in
1963. The car performed
faultlessly!*

riding on the crest of a wave; the Bavarian
State Mint even went so far as to issue
gold and silver coins to commemorate the
occasion. On one side they bore an outline
of the car, on the other an image of Heinz
Nordhoff. Volkswagen had become the
world's fourth (and on occasion third)
largest automobile manufacturer; only
Ford and General Motors were guaranteed
to out-produce them, with Chrysler
having to purchase Simca to ensure it
didn't slide down the ranking!

Wolfsburg, the Beetle's birthplace,
had grown to enormous proportions.
Spreading over 10.8 million square feet
in buildings alone, the factory was home
to in excess of 10,000 machines, and still
Nordhoff was insistent that more could
be achieved. Such was the demand for the
Beetle in North America that he decreed
an additional factory must be built to
cope with the ever-increasing strain put
upon Wolfsburg and its satellites by this
market. Hence 154.4 million DM were
invested in 1964 to build a new plant at
Emden, encompassing four halls and a
total of 140,000 square metres. Opening
its Palladian doors on 8 December, the
first car to be assembled there was hastily
dragged in front of the cameras, and
while it wasn't bedecked with flowers in
customary VW style, it did carry both the
appropriate registration plate EMD-78001
and a neatly prepared banner on its boot
lid, which read, '*der erste VW aus Emden
für Übersee*'. Initially, this assembly rather
than manufacturing factory produced 500
cars daily, each of which was despatched
from Volkswagen's own adjoining docks,
but within less than two years demand
ensured output had more than doubled to
1,100 vehicles.

The year following Emden's opening,
1965, proved to be significant in a number
of ways. This was the first occasion when
more than one million Beetles were
produced in a single 12-month period,
the year that saw the ten-millionth Beetle
rolled off the assembly line and bore
witness to the point when, for the first
time, Nordhoff relented to the pressure
placed on him by rival manufacturers and
allowed a larger engine to supplement the
faithful 34PS 1200.

After delivering 948,370 Beetles worldwide in 1964, production of the Beetle soared once more and in 1965 a grand total of 1,090,863 cars emerged from the various assembly lines across the world, with Wolfsburg supported by the recently opened factory at Emden carrying the lion's share of the load. Inevitably, with numbers of this kind emerging on a yearly basis more production milestones were set to tumble. From Nordhoff's appointment in January 1948 it had taken more than six-and-a-half years to amass the remaining numbers required for the Beetle to celebrate a million sales, while to achieve five million cars from a standing start had taken a little under 13 years. Now, within the space of just over three-and-a-half years, that number had been doubled, for the ten-millionth car rolled off the assembly line in September 1965. Fortuitously, the occasion coincided with the annual Frankfurt Motor Show and the event was relayed to crowds of gathered journalists, who, so it is said, burst into spontaneous applause. Generally regarded as cynical, renowned for dismissive critiques, and co-operatively condemnatory, the ovation they gave was recognition of the sense of fulfilment Nordhoff must have felt.

Continual improvement

For Nordhoff's Volkswagen it had been business as usual since the introduction of the 34PS engine in the summer of 1960. Cars produced after August 1961 featured a fuel gauge that was contained within its own separate housing to the left or right of the main dial dependent on whether the car was right- or left-hand drive, while worm and peg steering was made redundant in favour of an easier to operate worm and roller arrangement.

During the 1963 model year vinyl replaced cloth as the material used for the Beetle's headlining, and its introduction removed the habitual problem of rot around the rear window as the car grew older, a difficulty caused by excessive sunlight in some countries and by damp in rain-sodden Britain! On a more technical note, and strictly the preserve of those in the know about air-cooled cars, the Beetle was endowed with effective heat exchangers, thus dispensing with the old system of heater boxes that were prone to disgorge both exhaust and oil fumes into the interior of the car.

For 1964 cars one cost-cutting measure irritated Beetle fans beyond measure, although remedial action would take no longer than a couple of hours to complete. After a few years of painting the VW symbol on each hubcap in the body-colour of the car, Volkswagen had taken to etching out the letters in black, no matter what the paintwork finish of the vehicle. Now that luxury was also dispensed with! On a more serious level, sunroof models were endowed with an all-metal crank-operated panel as a replacement for the fold-back fabric roof that had been part of the model's make-up since its introduction in 1950. Partway through the model year, European-market vehicles were awarded a revised style of front indicator housing, which was both heftier in appearance and broader in width, the aim being to afford extra visibility.

In August 1964, the new '65 model year car could be instantly identified if placed next to older vehicles, for once again all the window sizes were increased. The windscreen was extended a further 28mm into the roof panel, while the rear window became larger by 20mm from top to bottom and by 10mm from left to right. To achieve increases in the side windows, the designers had taken their scalpels to the 'B' pillars, paring off sufficient metal to afford an 18 per cent increase in the size of the front side window, and a 6 per cent enlargement at the rear. With an 11 per cent enhancement to the overall size of the windscreen and a surprisingly large 20 per cent boost to the size of the rear window, the Beetle's interior was altogether lighter and airier, while visibility was similarly increased. Comparative trivialities, such as replacement of the old 'T' handle on the engine lid with a smaller and easier to operate push-button, demonstrated that Volkswagen continued to leave no stone unturned in carrying out Nordhoff's policy of continual improvement.

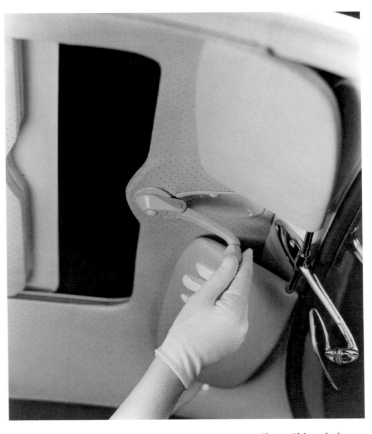

The VW 1300

Changes for the '66 model year, which came into play in August 1965, must have stunned many a student of Volkswagen's enduring philosophy.

Although adamant for many years that there was no need even to consider replacing the Beetle, Nordhoff was acutely aware of how sales of the Model T Ford suddenly tailed away, and how, for example, Citroën was deprived of a good proportion of its customer base when it had nothing to offer as a replacement for cars that had abruptly lost their popularity. Admittedly, with effect from the autumn of 1961, Nordhoff had a second string to his saloon bow, but the VW 1500 had never been intended to cater for the same market as the Beetle – this was a car for Beetle-owners with a growing family and a consequent need for more space to aspire to.

Above: Although the canvas sunroof first introduced in 1950 would linger on Standard models until the summer of 1967, for the '64 model year De Luxe cars were offered with a steel sliding roof operated by a retractable crank handle.

Right: By 1964, when this picture was taken, daily assembly at Wolfsburg stood at more than 4,000 cars.

Opposite: This Beetle publicity shot was intended to demonstrate just how popular Volkswagens were in the United States. With a little imagination at least nine Beetles and two Transporters can be picked out in this crowded New York street.

As a safeguard, rather than anything more serious, he ensured that the technical department was always occupied with possible Beetle replacements, even though the monotony of each car's rejection must have caused both Nordhoff and his designers an ever-growing sense of frustration.

With all such prototypes Nordhoff was certain of one issue: the overall size mustn't be greater than that of the Beetle. Rejecting one such vehicle presented to him for that very reason, he explained that 'if you make a car that is 50 centimetres longer, you add 100 kilograms to the weight. That means higher fuel consumption, but more importantly, most of all you need a bigger engine, and that takes you into a higher price bracket.'

Now, all of a sudden, in what appeared to be a complete volte-face, while the Beetle wasn't any longer or heavier than it had been before, for 1966 it came packaged with a larger engine. Volkswagen's irritation – to call it a problem would be to exaggerate its importance when production and sales were still forging ahead – was that newer cars from the stables of rival manufacturers were now consistently better performers than the Beetle, while the potential threat of Japanese expansion into Beetle territory across the world had to be countered before it gathered pace.

To achieve the much-vaunted 17½ per cent increase in power offered with the new engine, the VW 1500's crankshaft was utilised in the 1200 Beetle's crankcase, lengthening the stroke from 64mm to 69mm. This had the effect of giving an overall capacity of 1,285cc, while at the same time the compression ratio was raised from 7.0:1 to 7.3:1. A maximum of 40PS was achieved at 4,000rpm, an increase of 6PS over the 1200, affording both an all-day cruising and top speed of 76mph and an improved 0–60mph time, which, although rarely mentioned, had now come down to somewhere in the region of 23 seconds.

Nordhoff particularly was happy with the new engine, as it was far from radical in its concept and retained what was considered to be the company's dual hallmarks of longevity and reliability,

in that it continued to breathe through single-port heads, ensuring it remained under-stressed. The 1300 also met with the approval of the motoring press to the extent that Volkswagen's scrapbook of complimentary reviews must have been bursting at the seams. The much respected American magazine *Road and Track*, for example, not only heralded the arrival of the new engine with an article entitled 'More Bite for the Beetle', but peppered its content with Wolfsburg-endearing phrases such as 'a healthy increase in poke' and 'a difference in performance that is immediately discernible'. Although typically more staid in their approach, British magazines chorused a similar story. *Motor* wrote in congratulatory tones of the new Beetle's maximum speed, adding that 'acceleration' was 'now competitive with many rivals' and that the car had 'a new found urgency'. 'Through the gears,' it reported, 'the 1300 is appreciably quicker than the 1200 and

you don't need a stopwatch to detect the difference. In fact, acceleration is now comparable with cars like the BMC 1100, the Triumph Herald and the Hillman Imp, which hitherto had a comfortable edge over the VW.'

In the fever of emotion surrounding the increase in power few either noticed or cared to mention other changes. The addition of a 1300 badge on the engine compartment lid was pretty but of little value; the arrival of much better ventilated steel wheels, in the style of those fitted to the VW 1500 saloon, estate, and hatchback, was more important, as not only were the brakes more adequately cooled, but due to the large openings they were also lighter in weight. Aesthetics suffered, though, as the domed hubcaps of many years' standing gave way to a flat style, again previously the sole prerogative of the VW 1500, the larger Volkswagen saloon that had recently and so usefully evolved, chrysalis-like, into the VW 1600.

Right and above: To meet the ever-increasing demand for Beetles an additional factory was built at the port of Emden, where an ample supply of labour was available. From its inception the Emden plant fed the American market, and soon an 80-plus fleet of private charter ships was charged with transporting the Beetle across the Atlantic. The picture on the right dates from 1963.

This page: The 1965 model year Beetle's most noticeable refinement was the increase in glass size. The front screen (middle left), for example, extended a further 28 per cent into the roof panel. The cutaway image (middle right) indicates that changes had been made to the rear-seat backrest. The more detailed image (bottom right) confirms that it was now possible to fold the backrest right down. On a more trivial level, but confirming Volkswagen's continuing attention to detail, the sun-visors were redesigned (bottom left) and could be swivelled to the side.

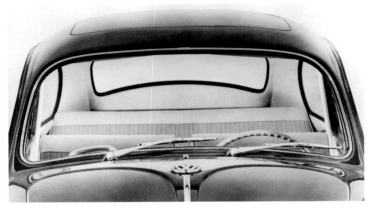

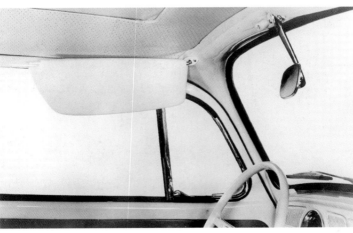

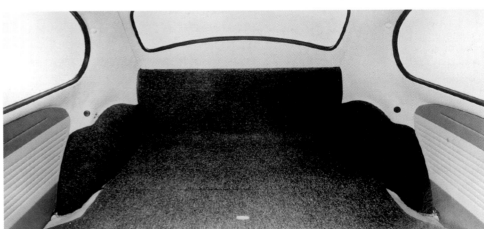

The VW 1500

Who would have thought it just a few short years ago? Exactly 12 months after launching the VW 1300, Nordhoff did it again and this time with a 1500 engine, a power unit destined to go down in Volkswagen's history as one of if not the best to power a Beetle. Such was the potential impact of the latest Beetle on the motoring world that the marketing department felt duty-bound to up the stakes and present the VW 1500 as the 'Hot VW'.

Out went the invitations to Volkswagen customers old and new to 'meet your new friend ... she's got a wide track, more powerful motor, equaliser spring and disc brakes ... [the] new hot VW 1500.'

Motoring journalists responded in a way that was extremely satisfying to Nordhoff, his management team, his dealer network, and countless salesmen. When magazines such as *Autosport*, a

Above and below: The new 1300 Beetle introduced for the '66 model year in August 1965 could be identified by a '1300' badge on the engine lid, ventilation slots in the wheels, and a new style of flat rather than domed hubcap, which was borrowed from the larger VW 1500.

title which normally concentrated on much beefier offerings than anything in Volkswagen's range, devoted extensive space to the VW 1500 there was no disguising their collective delight. The new car, the magazine purred, 'has appreciably more speed, very much better acceleration and a fuel consumption which is hardly any heavier'. Whether in the town, or out on the open road, the car was 'very nippy in traffic' and 'definitely lively'. The enthusiastic conclusion cancelled out any doubts in one or two minds that the Beetle's elderly design disqualified it from genuine praise. 'This new 1500 is sufficiently lively to be enjoyable to drive, and the handling and brakes now permit one to press on in safety.'

The progression from the 1300 of the '66 model year to the 1,493cc VW 1500 was entirely sound, as might be expected of Nordhoff's Volkswagen. The 1,285cc engine had given the Beetle a new set of legs, and the buying public's response had been universally favourable. The next logical step was to utilise the power of an engine already created, initially to power Volkswagen's larger saloon and more recently eased into the Transporter to give that vehicle the necessary get up and go the market would soon be demanding. Maximum power of 44PS at 4,000rpm was achieved by enlarging the bore from the 1300's 77mm to 83mm, while compression was increased from 7.3:1 to 7.5:1. Key to its success was more usable power across a much wider range – maximum torque of 78lb/ft was achieved at 2,600rpm.

Typically, Volkswagen quoted no more than 78mph as the top speed of the VW 1500, although many a driver found that speeds approaching the top end of the 80s were easily achievable and, thanks to other changes, were both safe and practical. Both the oft-quoted 0–50mph time of 13 seconds and the apparently leisurely 0–62mph sprint of 23 seconds were largely academic, as it was the way in which the VW 1500 could be driven, in part thanks to an array of other updates, that afforded the fun. The third gear ratio of all Beetles had been revised for the '67 model year to 1.26:1, while the VW 1500 Beetles benefited from a 4.125:1 rear axle ratio compared to the

Above and left: More or less concurrent with the introduction of the 1300 Beetle, the old Standard model received a makeover, becoming the 1200A. Painted bumpers and hubcaps and a lack of brightwork along the car's sides and around its windows confirmed its identity, although it now sported a 1200 badge on its engine lid. The eagle-eyed may be able to spot an ivory-coloured steering wheel in both images. The 1200 was dropped from the range in August 1966.

VW 1300's 4.375:1. A wider rear track, up from the 1200's 1,250mm of only a short time ago to 1,350mm, sat the vehicle more firmly on the ground. The fitting of an equaliser spring, which provided added assistance to the torsion bars when under load, and which was common to all models but of more obvious roadholding benefit in the largest-engined car, summarily eliminated a previous tendency to oversteer and cancelled any impediment to purposeful progress. The radical decision to add 277mm diameter disc brakes up front on the VW 1500 in place of the more staid if not necessarily boring drums, although not extended to US-bound cars, was also clearly intended to encourage a more lively driving style, as the possibility of locking the front wheels under heavy braking was significantly reduced.

For renowned author and German car expert Laurence Meredith to state unequivocally that nothing he drove from that period gave him so much satisfaction is praise indeed. Today, the '67 model year European Beetle is one of the most highly sought-after models, both for its classic looks – something that was set to

The deep but relatively short-lived recession of 1966 into 1967 led Nordhoff to reintroduce a financial crisis-orientated 1200 and market it as a budget Beetle – Der Sparkäfer. For Volkswagen it had the desired effect of increasing sales, albeit that the profit margin was not great.

change very shortly – and, of course, its performance. As for American 1500s, they gained 12-volt electrics, which raised a cheer or two, but lost the graceful lines of the front wings that melded so well with the equally refined shape of the car's headlamps, in favour of vertically set sealed-beam lights. Few would be unaware that this was to be the fate of all Beetles the following year, but in isolation to other changes they quite simply didn't look right. Brought about by burgeoning state legislation, a demand from the same irritating source for an amendment at the car's rear, and one that was applied to European models too, fortunately gave the car a tweak in its appearance that suited its beefier performance. Few would have envisaged that in satisfying a demand that the Beetle's rear registration plate should sit virtually vertically on the engine lid, the resultant humped metal would give the impression of more meat and more purpose lurking beneath it.

Right: Volkswagen's press picture gave few clues that here there was a new 'Hot Beetle'.

1968–1978 NEW BEETLES

The start of the '68 model year and the launch of a Beetle sufficiently revised in its appearance to justify the marketing gurus' banner headings proclaiming *Die Neuen Käfer*, coupled to both a boost in production fortunes and attendant export figures, should have spelled no less than success for Volkswagen, and guaranteed enduring longevity for the Beetle. However, ill-fortune lay just around the corner, for in April 1968 Nordhoff died. The security of 20 years of considered, highly successful management was gone, while the Beetle, the company's core product, lost its greatest protagonist.

Over the next four years, and despite the appearance of a completely new type of Beetle in the form of the MacPherson-strut, big-booted 1302, Volkswagen's profitability spiralled rapidly downhill, a direct result of poor policy direction from one Kurt Lotz, Nordhoff's successor and the undoubted villain of any tale concerning *Der Käfer*. The good news for Volkswagen, after Lotz had been reminded that his contract was not infinite and that he was accountable for his failures, was that the upper echelons ensured that a more determined, far-thinking, professional motor manufacturer was appointed in his place. However, for the Beetle this was not a guarantee of future security.

Rudolph Leiding was destined to oversee the arrival of the day that the Beetle pushed the Model T Ford into second position in terms of total automobile production. He sanctioned continuation of the project to take the MacPherson-strut Beetle's development one stage further, but he also ruthlessly set in place a strategy to replace it as quickly as possible. 1974 saw the first serious tumble in production numbers; the Beetle was banished from Wolfsburg to allow its successor to take prime position. From this point until the long-dreaded day in January 1978 when German Beetle saloon production finished forever the car's story was one of dwindling sales, reduced model options, and mounting depression for its followers.

Right: Several hallmarks of the '68 model year abound in the press pictures. Sturdier 'U'-profile bumpers set higher on the car, a stubbier engine lid, revised rear valance, and larger rear light clusters, all made the new car instantly recognisable.

Right: Further hallmarks of the '68 model year are apparent in this shot of the 'new Beetle' from the front. Vertically set headlamps, bumpers set higher on the car, a stubbier boot lid and revised front valances changed the stature of the car.

Below: The Cabriolet followed where the saloon led, and since the introduction of the 1300 back in August 1965 carried the most powerful engine available. (Some exceptions to this rule emerged in the 1970s for selected markets, primarily linked to tax laws.)

The 'new' Beetle

Concurrent with the launch of an all-new Transporter, and theoretically silencing Nordhoff's would-be critics who were eager to pronounce him incapable of changing models, cars produced from August 1967 made their predecessors of just months earlier appear outdated. The Beetle had a new, more aggressive, worldly-wise stance.

At the latest model's front end the US-specification only innovation of August 1966 – vertically set headlamps on reshaped wings – became the blueprint for all future Beetles. The top of the range 1500 and its sibling 1300 were given distinctive U-profile chromed bumpers adorned with a decorative softening strip of black tape running along the lightly indented, rigidity enhancing central horizontal plane. The new bumpers were also set higher on the body, a move that required the pressing of a revised stubbier boot lid and production of a reshaped front valance, both of which had the effect of updating the Beetle's classic lines. At the rear the new bumper demanded a squarer, chunkier style of engine compartment lid in keeping with its counterpart at the front and a similarly revised valance. New, larger and consequently more dominant, prominently segmented and trimmed light clusters sat on redefined wings. Simple, but strikingly effective, these changes were the essence of the new Beetle, although, as might be anticipated from a firm renowned for its attention to detail, many other minor changes were made.

As examples of the practical and illustrations of the aesthetic, none of which really hit the headlines, the brackets that supported the new bumpers were considerably more robust in their construction, while the decorative horn grille positioned towards the bottom of the front nearside wing and the attendant balancing dummy on the offside wing were deleted as symbols of outdated styling. Similarly, although not evident until the car was in use, a much requested enhancement of the candle-like six-volt electric system to the industry's near norm of 12 volts – previously the exclusive prerogative of US owners since

Above and left: The arrival in September 1967 of the externally virtually indistinguishable semi-automatic Beetle was a move designed primarily with the American market in mind. Somewhat leisurely in its performance, and particularly so when fitted with the 1300 engine (one year into general production), the semi-automatic had one great advantage over other Beetles: double-joined drive-shafts enabled drivers to take corners faster without the danger of rear wheels tucking in. Launch publicity images depicted the 'new' model against the factory's restored 1938 KdF-Wagen.

August 1966 – was both a practical and a
significant move. The previously somewhat
restricted flow of fresh air through the
car was enhanced by the inclusion of boot
lid louvres that allowed air into a plastic
box behind the dash, from where it was
fed through flexible pipes to dashboard
vents, resulting in a more satisfactory,
fresher feel for both driver and passengers.
Gone too were the days when it was
necessary to lift the boot lid to locate the
petrol filler for refuelling; this was now
concealed behind a little flap in the right-
hand front quarter-panel. Inside the car,
the fuel gauge was incorporated into the
single combination instrument, ridding
the dashboard of a device that looked as
if it was added as an afterthought, while
the ignition 'switch' position was moved

from an inconvenient arm-stretching
location on the dash to an altogether more
suitable site on the steering column, which
was itself improved so that thanks to
incorporation of a lattice section it would
collapse in the event of the driver hitting it
during an accident.

Whether aesthetically as graceful or
not, the '68 model year 1500 Cabriolet and
Saloon and the 1300 were significantly
better Beetles than previously. A further
innovation, deliberately introduced to
accommodate the preferences of many
American drivers, was the arrival of a semi-
automatic Beetle in September 1967, a car
that was initially based solely on the 1500
model. Fitted with a three-speed gearbox,
its ratios corresponding to second, third,
and fourth on a manual car, this model –

known as the 'Stickshift' Bug in the USA
– was possessed of a conventional clutch
with a torque converter. Although not fully
automatic, as it was necessary to use the
stubby gear lever to change ratio either
up or down, it was eminently practical
to engage ratio two, start off at the most
leisurely of paces and retain the setting for
the rest of the day.

Undoubtedly the greatest asset of the
semi-automatic's specification was the
adoption of completely new, technically
sophisticated, double-jointed rear swing-
axles that were no longer contained within
tubes. As this offered uniform roadholding
characteristics whatever the load, the
result was a vast reduction in the well-
known tendency of the Beetle to tuck its
wheels under when cornering hard.

Consequences of Nordhoff's final years and his death

'It was during this period ... [when] VW's main competitive advantage – the mass production of one model – ... threatened to become an ominous disadvantage ... that the Heinrich Nordhoff era ended. He held firmly on to the Volkswagen saloon, which during his lifetime was perfected into the technically mature Beetle, as well as on the combination of mass production and the global market orientation, leading the Volkswagenwerk to the pinnacle of the European automobile industry. In order to maintain this position far-reaching changes were necessary after Nordhoff's death...' – Markus Lupa, *Volkswagen Chronicle* volume 7, Volkswagen AG Corporate History Department.

Although written in a way intended to lull the reader into a false sense of security by adding compliments to subtle criticism, few will be beguiled into thinking that the official Volkswagen line concerning the end of the Nordhoff era and the company's subsequent trials and tribulations has changed. Established in the late 1960s, when it proved expedient to blame Nordhoff for shortcomings not of his making, this fable remains embedded in Volkswagen's annals. Here the intention is to clear Nordhoff's name and to offer the Beetle a reprieve, as the two go hand in hand.

Nordhoff reached the customary retirement age of 65 in January 1964, and while there had been occasional mumbles from sections of the motoring press and elsewhere that he should replace the Beetle nobody took them seriously enough to suggest that the director general might give way to a younger man unless he chose to. Nordhoff himself made it abundantly clear that it was his intention to carry on, and when in 1965 Beetle production topped the one-million mark in a 12-month period for the first time the great man's standing rose even higher, if that was possible.

However, 1966 saw the onset of the first real recession in Germany since Hitler's defeat. Volkswagen had been integral to the economic miracle of the 1950s and remained so, and as such would be the subject of careful scrutiny if circumstances changed. At the start of 1966 the company had negotiated the biggest wage contracts in its history; so significant were they that the prices of all models, including the Beetle, had to be adjusted. Unfortunately, this increase coincided with the downturn, and soon – in common with other manufacturers – Volkswagen was amassing stockpiles of unsold new vehicles on its dealer forecourts.

Reluctant to condemn his workforce to short hours, or worse still to make a percentage redundant, for once Nordhoff procrastinated. He was also aware that if he cut production he would hardly serve the cause of the German government, as the nation would realise that if Volkswagen had to cut back then the recession must be serious. However, by the start of 1967 Nordhoff recognised that to retain Volkswagen's essential and commendable level of profitability adjustments had to be made. Whereas US-owned Ford and Opel both served writs of mass redundancy on their respective workforces to meet what was now a market slump, Nordhoff protected his workforce to the best of his ability by instating short working weeks and by introducing what was quickly nicknamed the *Sparkäfer*, or budget Beetle. The basic 1200 that emerged served several purposes: it kept production

Left: Kurt Lotz, Nordhoff's successor. His tenure in office was mercifully short, but catastrophic for the Beetle and dangerous to Volkswagen's overall wellbeing.

workers at least partly gainfully employed; it generated sales to people who recognised a bargain when it was placed before them; and it engendered the right feelings for, and enhanced the profile of, the Beetle. Building it wasn't the most profitable of exercises and on this issue Nordhoff turned on the recently elected coalition government.

Below: The 1970 model year Beetle for the American market was fitted with a 1600 engine borrowed from the second-generation Transporter. The press release accompanying this image referred to 'more rapid acceleration in the lower ranges of its four-speed synchromesh transmission'. Note also the side reflector on the rear light cluster and the exceptionally large indicator on the front wings – both features unique to the North American market.

This page: 'The new Volkswagen 1600 Super Beetle is the latest addition to the top-selling Beetle range. It can be recognised by its "pregnant look" – the longer deeper front, larger hump of the engine compartment cover, and louvres behind the rear windows for the through-flow ventilation.' – Public relations department, Volkswagen Motors Ltd.

To Nordhoff's dismay Bonn did little to assist the motor industry in such difficult times, rather it opted to make matters worse. Firstly petrol taxes were raised, secondly automobile insurance rates were allowed to spiral upwards, and thirdly, crucially, the government slashed in half the tax concession German workers benefited from if they drove their cars, Beetle or otherwise, to and from work.

At this point Nordhoff made a fatal mistake, one undoubtedly caused by the cult of infallibility built around him and for him by his press department, the function of which for many years had been to enhance sales of the product he had championed – the Beetle. Knowingly or unknowingly, Nordhoff had become the king of Wolfsburg, and as such he felt he could speak with impunity. His word, or so he thought, had become law. Suitably bolstered, he spoke out forcefully against what he considered to be a string of short-sighted measures at the heart of government policy with regard to the automobile industry. Instead of the quick fixes devised by Bonn, he advocated the abolition of car registration tax and a reduction in vehicle ownership levies, both of which moves, he believed, would aid not only Volkswagen's cause but those of all other manufacturers directly and indirectly related to the motor industry.

In so doing Nordhoff created an enemy in the form of the government's jovially bombastic Finance Minister, Franz-Josef Strauss. Cornered, Strauss retaliated in more ways than one. He variously attacked Volkswagen, and by clear implication Nordhoff, with accusations ranging from 'hoarding up vast financial reserves over many years' and producing 'too many cars and too few ideas', through to condemnation of their product with remarks such as 'two glorious initials on the bonnet of a car don't make up for the lack of comfort', and the more succinct one of building 'the wrong models'. Criticism was also expressed via sections of the media sympathetic to his cause – *Bild* newspaper simply declaring that 'VW has been asleep'. Aware that despite prolific production and, at least until the recession, an ever-increasing volume of

sales, the home market had experienced something of a decline as challengers Ford and Opel tailored models offering more in the way of both space and performance than the Beetle's elderly design could hope to achieve, Strauss made a further attack by asking what would happen 'when the USA stop being amused by the Beetle?'

While Nordhoff could easily respond to such blasts from Strauss by pointing out that 68 per cent of exports didn't go to America, so that even in the highly unlikely scenario of the USA stopping buying the Beetle overnight Volkswagen could survive, the damage had still been done.

Although Nordhoff had hinted that he would retire at the beginning of 1969, just a few days short of his 70th birthday, no definite plans had been made. What remained clear was that he wished to select his successor and that he wanted to retain influence by heading the company's supervisory board thereafter. While such bodies were and are commonplace in Germany, Volkswagen's was a little different in that it contained equal representation from the Bonn government and the state of Lower Saxony, within whose boundaries Wolfsburg lay, as well as worker representatives and management members. In theory, this was the body whose role had been developed to encompass the appointment of a replacement director general when the time came. On 29 June 1966 industrialist Josef Rust had been appointed chairman of this board, and it now became apparent that this former aide to Franz-Josef Strauss welcomed the opportunity to add a dual task to his role – that of forcing Nordhoff to retire as soon as possible, and of ensuring that his successor was of an appropriate political persuasion.

In that second aim Rust was successful. Carl Hahn – Nordhoff's protégé of the mid-1950s and, more recently, the highly successful head of Volkswagen of America from 1959 to 1964 – had been recalled to Wolfsburg as king in waiting. In the interim Nordhoff had bestowed upon him responsibility for worldwide sales and service, revelling in the attributes of his Americanisation and the consequent understanding of the Beetle being an

international commodity. Walter Henry Nelson attributed the following words to Nordhoff: 'We take our promising men and send them out into the field to test them before we bring them home.'

Hahn's time at VWoA had left a glittering trail. It was he, as we have seen, who had chosen the innovative advertising agency DDB to promote the Beetle in the United States, and had staved off the challenge of 'home-grown' product; it was Hahn who overviewed the arrival of the millionth Beetle in America in 1962, and the following year led VWoA to the pole position of capturing nearly 70 per cent of the imported car market, with sales of 240,000 vehicles, a result which justified increasing the number of US dealers from 687 to 744. By the time of his recall to Germany during the latter part of 1964 the new factory at Emden was nearing completion, a complex constructed specifically to cater with the pressures placed on Volkswagen at Wolfsburg and Hanover to meet the demands of the American market.

So obvious was Hahn's allegiance to Nordhoff that Rust manipulated him not only out of the race but, to Volkswagen's cost, eventually out of the company too. Fortune played into the hands of the conspirators, for at this crucial time Nordhoff's health began to deteriorate. From December 1966 colleagues noticed a growing irritability, increased impatience and, most seriously, a remarkable lack of appetite. Nordhoff struggled on as might be anticipated of this workaholic, but at the age of 68 it appeared entirely acceptable for Rust to bring forward the appointment of a deputy, and when in May 1967 Nordhoff suffered what has been variously described as a severe heart and circulatory attack, or simply a sharp decline, the imminent appointment of one Kurt Lotz was vindicated.

Lotz was an industrialist who had worked his way through the ranks to the position of director general of Brown, Boveri et Cie, a large Swiss-owned engineering firm. Conveniently both Rust and a fellow supervisory board member, Hermann Richter, were on the board of BBC and were aware that the ambitious Lotz would toe the line if Nordhoff could be prised out of his position. All seemed oblivious to the fact that Lotz was a complete novice as far as the automobile industry was concerned, or, alternatively, opted to disregard this all too serious defect in their appointee's make-up.

After spending time at a sanatorium in Zürich, Nordhoff returned to work in the autumn of 1967, but it was apparent to all that he had some way to go before making a full recovery; speech proved difficult, and increasing deafness deprived him of the ability to follow all the conversations that it was vital he should hear. On 6 January 1968, the occasion of his 69th birthday, the barely recognisable Nordhoff made the famous speech where he foresaw the Beetle's star shining brightly for many years to come, extracts of which have been presented earlier in this book. At least one member of his audience did not share such a view. Two months later Rust and his colleagues imparted the news to Nordhoff that his retirement had been brought forward to 21 May 1968. From that point, almost as if to prove that he was both invincible and irreplaceable, Nordhoff exerted himself to the full. On 15 March 1968, on the way back from Baden-Baden where he had rushed to make yet another speech, Nordhoff collapsed. He died in Wolfsburg's hospital on 12 April surrounded by members of his family.

The Lotz years

In the hands of Nordhoff's successor the Beetle faced an uncertain future despite apparently record-breaking figures of more than one kind. At face value, with the recession of late 1966 and 1967 over in Germany and other countries, and a substantially revised car on offer, the prospects should have been good. Production numbers, which had fallen to 925,787 in 1967 after two years when they had exceeded a million cars, had bounced back to 1,186,134 vehicles in 1968 and were set to hover at this level or slightly higher for the next few years, eventually peaking in 1971 – the last year of Lotz's tenure – at a massive 1,291,612 Beetles. Similarly, sales in the United States had rocketed to an all-time high in 1968 when 423,008 Beetles were first registered for use on American roads.

The one statistic, however, that served as confirmation that all was not well for the Beetle was the most important one of all; the one that indicated the viability of Volkswagen as a company – its record of profitability. In 1968, Lotz inherited and possibly even contributed to a profit of 339 million DM for Volkswagen AG. Few were concerned about the slight drop to a mere 330 million DM in 1969, but when in 1970 the figure had tumbled to 190 million warning bells began to sound, and a year later forecasts of a tiny profit of no more than 12 million DM played no small part in the decision to oust Lotz in favour of someone who understood the car-manufacturing business.

Within months if not weeks of Nordhoff's death Lotz was speaking of Volkswagen having been 'immovable under a single director for the past 20 years'. Now, he told any audience willing to listen to him, the only way forward was to destroy the past as quickly as possible: 'we had to move from monolith to a many-faceted product'. Lotz spoke openly of Volkswagen's 'only chance for survival' being a 'new car'. He was even quite happy to manipulate the truth to suit his cause, placating Beetle fans by suggesting the car still 'maintained its attractions' before perpetrating the myth that its 'impact' was 'tending to die down in some markets'.

By 24 April 1969, when he was interviewed by *The Autocar* magazine, he had come to believe that his lack of knowledge outweighed experience spanning more than four decades. His repetitive portrayal of Volkswagen as a rigid to the point of destruction one-model company was by now inextricably linked to the dismissal of Nordhoff as an absolute dictator. Lotz told the magazine that Volkswagen had 'diversified and instead of offering a single range we have adopted a strategy of parallel divisions', although tangible evidence of such a strategy had yet to be seen. To implement such a policy he was proud and confident to announce that he had been forced to rid himself of the majority of Nordhoff's management

Right: 'MacPherson-type front suspension on Volkswagen's new 1971 Super Beetle uses progressive coil springs to smooth the ride, eliminates the need for periodic front-end lubrication. Two universal joints in safety steering column help limit rearward movement of the column in the event of a frontal collision.' – Volkswagen of America Inc.

team within less than 12 months of the original director general's death. 'On 31st December last year, the average age of our board was 62. A few months later, following a number of retirements, it was down to 47. Now only one of my colleagues is older than myself ... It is superfluous for me to refer to the effects of this rejuvenation on the form as a whole.'

Lotz's perception of his role at Volkswagen was clear: he believed, and rightly, that he had been appointed for the purpose of axing the Beetle from the range. He would throw the experience and knowledge of the last 20 years to one side. At a time when total Beetle production stood at the brink of tens of millions, he categorically stated that 'Wolfsburg will never see the 20 million mark ... we won't repeat Ford's mistake.' As history came to demonstrate, the ways in which Lotz opted to bring about a new Volkswagen were wrong on every conceivable count.

Lotz was wrong to appoint Werner Holste to take over the technical reigns at Wolfsburg. While he considered it a positive bonus that Holste wasn't in any way connected with Volkswagen's past, he, like Lotz, lacked the relevant expertise

and knowledge, coming instead from a background of general mechanical engineering. Likewise, if his aim was to destroy the Beetle as quickly as possible and to replace it with something equally capable of making substantial profits for the company, he was wrong to waste his years in office wavering between a succession of curious prototypes largely designed and produced for him by Porsche without taking decisive action in favour of any of them.

Unquestionably Lotz was wrong in his choice of the one model he launched that he might call his own. Briefly, as this is the story of the Beetle and not one of Volkswagen generally, Lotz's only contribution to the model range was the K70, the company's first and unquestionably disastrous dabble into water-cooling. In January 1965 Volkswagen had gained a controlling interest in Auto Union; now, under Lotz, the battle was fought to add NSU to the company's portfolio. In the spring of 1969 NSU were ready to launch a model they had been developing for the last three years; pre-release press drives had taken place, and stand space had been booked at the forthcoming Geneva Motor Show. Suddenly,

everything was cancelled. The acquisition of NSU by Volkswagen meant that Lotz wanted to launch the car as his own. While the K70's dull, uncompromising, three-box shape promised less than beneficial anonymity, producing an appallingly bad drag coefficient of 0.51 and in turn guaranteeing heavy fuel consumption, it was its catalogue of other faults, including poor engine reliability and overheating, that made it like no other Volkswagen. Lurking behind the scenes, but unknown at its launch, premature excessive rusting set it apart from the classic models. Determined that it would sell, Lotz pitched the K70 at a price below that of the Audi 100, allowing himself a negligible profit of just 33DM per car, while he rounded on the VW 411 – the last of the air-cooled models conceived in the Nordhoff era but launched after his death, and potentially another rival to the K70 in terms of size and performance – describing it as 'no metal Adonis'.

Amazingly, when what has been written of Lotz is taken into consideration, it was during his tenure of office that the most radical development in the Beetle's lengthy history occurred.

Left: Was the 1302's comparatively cavernous boot its greatest asset?

This page: Although the new Super Beetles dominated the headlines, Volkswagen still offered torsion-bar Beetles. The 1971 model 1300 (right) benefited from through ventilation, as denoted by the crescent-shaped vents behind the rear side-window, while ten cooling louvres (below left) were cut into the engine lid, previously a preserve of the 1500 Beetle and now part of the 1302's make-up. The 1200 (below right) had soldiered on almost unchanged since the '68 model year. Note the indentation in the metal behind the rear side-window, which was new for the '71 model year, as were headlamps that switched off when the ignition was turned off, a larger windscreen washer bottle, and towing eyes front and rear.

The 1302 – the Super Beetle

Why Lotz decided to invest heavily in the very model he wished to rid Volkswagen of will forever remain a mystery. He was certainly aware that an upsurge in legislation in the United States designed to make all cars safer for their occupants – in essence a forerunner of the all-pervasive health and safety legislation we all suffer under today – threatened the very existence of such an old design as that of the Beetle, but his 1970 introduction offered nothing more in this respect than had the 'New Beetle' of August 1967 during the Nordhoff era. And why, if he had decided that the car should be modernised in one final fling before it was cast aside forever, did he also retain most of the original line-up of Beetle models? Perhaps the new car was simply another example of woolly strategy; a vehicle epitomised by its unusual branding, a compromise that satisfied nobody.

The first step towards the introduction of the 1302 Beetle had come only 12 months earlier and, being a result of demands made in the USA, was restricted to the American market. The briefest of press releases accompanying imagery of the 1970 model year car stated that 'Volkswagen's 1970 Beetle sedan features a slightly larger engine giving it greater response and more rapid acceleration in the lower ranges of its four-speed synchromesh transmission...'

Even the befuddled Lotz wouldn't have gone to the expense of developing a power unit exclusive to one market; instead he responded to ongoing demands for extra performance by borrowing the relatively recently launched engine that had been placed in the second generation Transporter from that vehicle's inception in August 1967. The 1,584cc engine came with a bore and stroke of 85.5mm and 69mm respectively, and a compression ratio of 7.7:1, while maximum power of 47PS was achieved at 4,000rpm. Maximum torque of 103Nm occurred at just 2,200rpm, even better than that of the outgoing 1500 and guaranteeing usable power across an even wider range. Perhaps inevitably an exhaust gas purification

system was fitted, a feature which had the effect of detracting slightly from the vehicle's performance. Externally, the latest model was recognisable by two banks of five horizontal louvres carved into the engine lid of the saloon, and an increase in the number of the same additional cooling device on the cabriolet, which now totalled 28 in four banks of seven. Although strictly unnecessary, European 1500 models acquired the same distinguishing marks.

Before any statement or description concerning the 1302 Beetle can be made, its designation demands an explanation. Why, for example, wasn't the new model given a VW 1600 badge, as both the 1,285cc and 1,493cc models before it had been, at least for the European market? The answer came with the knowledge that the original style of Beetle, presented until then in 1500, 1300, and 1200 guise, was not to be replaced, or at least the latter two models weren't; the new car was either to supplement them or, more realistically, to take their respective places at the top of the range. As the new car was

to be offered with both a 1300 and 1600 engine, somewhat crazy logic demanded that they be called the 1301 and 1301S respectively, the 'S' device already being in use in conjunction with the larger air-cooled cars in production and intended to denote a higher powered engine. However, a technical hitch remained, in that the French company Simca already had a 1301 on their books. The only option then was to refer to the latest Beetles as a 1302 if the model carried a 1300 engine and as a 1302S if a 1600 engine was installed. Clearly someone forgot to take into account that the 1302 was nowhere near as widely available as its bigger-engined brother, with, for example, both the USA and Britain not taking the former model.

Fortunately, common sense prevailed in marketing circles at least, in that they christened the new car the 'Super Beetle', although whether the rest of an oft-used message met the necessary standards set in advertising is open to question. Perhaps the strapline 'The most powerful, most exciting and most comfortable Beetle ever' should have been amended to add 'and

Below: This colourful image of the Beetle assembly line from 1971, when yearly Beetle production peaked at 1,291,612 cars, forms a suitable prelude to a series of images designed to offer a virtual tour of Beetle manufacture – from panel pressing to export.

Opposite: Wolfsburg circa 1971 – note the growth since the picture on page 99, taken a little over a decade earlier.

Far left: The automated presses controlled by just one man from a control desk.

Left: A continually moving conveyor belt carried the parts from machine to machine.

Left: A giant carousel revolved 210 times per hour and formed the Beetle's front sections with 258 spot welds.

Right: All the necessary parts came to each carousel automatically. Pictured here is the machinery used to form the Beetle's rear sections.

Right: The body assembly line consisted of a 590ft-long bank of coupled machines capable of producing 300 Beetle bodies every day.

Far right: Fully automated: each section of the Beetle is carried by conveyer belt to the next. The picture shows the roof panels being gathered to meet the already mated front and rear sections. From here the body went on a high line conveyor where sealing welds were carried out.

Far left: Before painting, the Beetle's body was washed for 25 minutes and then dried for eight minutes. After immersion in a tank of primer the first coat of paint was applied by the electrophoresis method, best described as akin to chromium plating. Next followed electrostatic application of the undercoat, giving the paintwork both its thickness and its durability. Finally, the finishing coat was applied by workers using hand-held guns for a perfect finish. The car's paintwork was then baked hard in high-temperature ovens.

Top right: The Hanover factory was responsible for building the Beetle's engine and adding heat exchangers, silencers, and dynamos, before bench-testing each unit prior to its despatch to Wolfsburg. Daily production in 1971 averaged in excess of 4,000 units.

Left: After painting, the cars were conveyed to a series of parallel trim lines where tasks ranging from the insertion of wiring looms to the fixing of brightwork strips and the fitting of linings were carried out.

certainly the most controversial and ugly creation to date'!

The single most striking feature of the 1302 was the dramatic alteration in its facial appearance compared to that of the original Beetle, a change brought about by making Ferdinand Porsche's legendary rugged torsion-bar suspension redundant at the front. In its place aficionados were presented with conventional MacPherson struts which, according to the publicity blurb, had the effect of 'smoothing the ride' while 'eliminating the need for front-end lubrication'. This rudimentary change in specification inevitably meant that towers had to be built to house the coil springs, which in turn had the effect of altering the shape of the wings, making them more bulbous in appearance and the 1302 more frog-eyed in its looks.

Possibly Lotz's real purpose in spending the many million DM it took to develop the concept was a worthwhile increase in what had admittedly been cramped boot space. With the 1302 capacity went from 140 litres/4.9cu ft to 260 litres/9.2cu ft, or a startling 85 per cent increase, which in part was due to being able to lay the spare

tyre flat below the lower section of a two-step boot. The reason for the existence of the step in the first place was the location and concealment of the fuel tank – just imagine if this necessary commodity could have been banished to another area of the car what the effect would have been.

Unfortunately, a result of this feverish design activity was that the boot lid became much larger too, contributing to a 74mm/3in increase in the car's overall length, a side-view inspection revealing the car's new and decidedly unattractive humped appearance. Viewed from the front the 1302 looked even less eye-catching, the bloated expanse of the boot lid leading many to describe the car as 'the pregnant Beetle'.

However, to say that the 1302 was a complete disaster would be wrong, for at its rear end it benefited from the previously exclusive preserve of the semi-automatic and America-bound saloons in that it possessed revised rear swing axles, which were double-jointed in nature and no longer contained within torsion tubes. The result was that under hard cornering conditions the car was far less likely to tuck a rear wheel under itself, and therefore proved

altogether safer than the straightforward torsion bars models, particularly if an enthusiastic driver who liked to take bends at speed was at the wheel. Perhaps it is worth adding as a side note that the front disc brakes bestowed on the 1500 Beetle were carried forward to the 1302S, but inevitably the 1302, like its torsion-bar counterpart the 1300, operated with drums.

Although not exclusive to the 1302 range, the introduction of new 1300 and 1600 engines enhanced the Beetle's performance. Gone were the single port engines of old in all models save the 1200, which as might have been inferred remained delightfully antiquated. In their place were units that had revised cylinder heads with twin inlet ports per head – a sure means of allowing an engine to breathe more easily. The result was a welcome if relatively modest increase in power, the smaller 1,285cc engine now offering 44PS at 4,100rpm and the 1,584cc delivering 50PS at 4,000rpm, a goodly increase on the old 1500 engine and better than the US-market-only 1600 engine already described. Deftly, Volkswagen's marketing men referred to

Left: Upon receipt of the necessary component parts, the chassis, engine, axles, and transmission moved along to meet finished bodies as they descended from a roofline conveyer. Bolted together automatically, the finishing touches came with the addition of a fuel tank, steering gear, and wheels. Close to the end of the assembly line the Beetle received its seats and finally three litres of fuel so that it could be driven on to a roller test stand.

Right: Each car's worthiness was put to the test on the roller station. A driver accelerated the engine through its gears to a speed equivalent to 60mph. Instruments assessed exhaust emissions, and brakes had to be proven effective and even in application.

Far right: Almost all the Beetles produced at Wolfsburg left the factory by rail, averaging 60 trains per day, each of which carried 300 cars on two-tier transporters and totalled 650 yards in length.

Right: Each special ship assigned to the export of Beetles could carry 3,000 vehicles. The ports at Emden and Bremen served the American markets. Most UK-bound Beetles also came from Emden, but some originated in Antwerp. Beetles destined for Scandinavia departed from Lübeck. Exports to other parts of the world, including the Middle and Far East, Africa, Australia, and South America, were sent via regular shipping operations.

the performance of the 1302S in terms of 0–50mph, rather than the more normal 0–60, where a less than earth-shattering time of 12.5 seconds was given. Better news came in the form of the 1302S model's maximum speed, which now stood at a figure in excess of 80mph for the first time.

Lotz clearly thought the benefits of the twin-port engines outweighed any potential problems; it is probable that Nordhoff would have considered otherwise. In terms of longevity the latest power plants created an unprecedented level of disappointment and surprise; dreadful flat-spots were one cause of

notoriety, while cracked cylinder heads were quite simply not compatible with the quality of Volkswagens of the Nordhoff era. Perhaps Lotz had been hoodwinked through his inexperience. A cheap course of action had been taken – boring a second hole in each head was not comparable with designing a brand new engine, but then neither was the expense involved.

Press and public reaction to the 1302 range was less than euphoric, many of the former comparing it unfavourably with the latest offerings from rival manufacturers, while the loyal Volkswagen-purchasing 'come what may' element of the latter

simply preferred the torsion-bar models. But more than anything it was the look of the 1302 range that let it down; its appearance, and in reality its revised chassis that offered better roadholding but not necessarily better handling, quite simply wasn't a part of the established cult of the Beetle. A hidden negative, though one that would be only too apparent to any accountant, was that the extensive nature of the new panels and pressings required to complete the 1302 inevitably made it the most costly revision to any model of Beetle in its history, something Lotz was seemingly oblivious to.

Panic measures set in place before Lotz's departure

As the storm clouds gathered over Lotz's mercifully brief tenure as director general one issue panicked him into taking a step that would add to the financial burdens placed on Volkswagen's already tottering bank balance. Secretly admitting that he was no nearer finding a replacement for the Beetle than when he first assumed high office, something had to be done to address the very real concern that within a short time the Beetle wouldn't be saleable in the United States. The issue, of course, was one of the curses of mankind – state legislation at its most meddlesome.

Rules and regulations that demanded the standardisation of bumper heights between European built and Detroit-assembled vehicles may have been a contributory factor in the reshaping of

the Beetle in 1967, as might have been the larger and arguably uglier rear light clusters of the same period. No doubt to the intense annoyance of the do-gooders who were convinced that such an elderly design could not be permitted to grace US highways any longer, the Beetle passed potentially crippling new sets of laws concerning petrol spillage in the case of a head-on collision with flying colours, but there was something far more dangerous lurking in the wings of pedantic bureaucracy. There was a distinct possibility that a law would be devised stipulating a minimum distance between the driver or front-seat passenger and the windscreen. A result of the introduction of the 1302 might have been to increase the distance between the occupants of such a car and the

vehicle in front, but that was not the issue. The equivalent of a British green paper confirmed that if what was planned became law, the Beetle could not comply.

With immediate effect Lotz commissioned work to save the day. The result was the most un-Beetle-like Beetle ever, a car with a distinctive curved windscreen and – horror of horrors to the purists – a moulded plastic dashboard. Cut and sliced into the Macpherson strut technology of the 1302 and launched ten months to the day after Lotz's back-door departure, this was the 1303 Beetle. As befits the topsy-turvy nature of the four years with Lotz at the helm, Volkswagen needn't have bothered developing the 1303, as the proposed regulation that panicked its birth never came into effect.

Rudolph Leiding, the most maligned of all director generals

Like his predecessor, Rudolph Leiding would stay at the helm of Volkswagen for no more than four years, and to the casual observer with an eye for figures it is easy to see why. From Lotz's final snivelling year when, as has already been recorded, Volkswagen made just 12 million DM profit, Leiding appeared to start off well. In 1972 the company recorded an 86 million DM profit and the following year that increased to 109 million. However, in 1974 such apparent success had turned into a dramatic 555 million DM *loss*, and

even after Leiding had 'retired' at the start of 1975 a substantial loss remained, the deficit amounting to 145 million DM. On the other hand his successor, ex-Ford man Toni Schmücker, would record a profit of 784 million DM in 1976, a figure even Nordhoff couldn't equal. Clearly Leiding was an out-and-out failure. Or was he?

A diehard Beetle enthusiast has no reason to love Rudolph Leiding; but anyone who drives a modern Volkswagen in the 21st century has. For it was Leiding and none other who ousted the Beetle

from Wolfsburg as the pivotal vehicle of Volkswagen's success, and it was his ruthless determination that would see Volkswagen rise from the ashes of one of the worst crises the automotive world has ever seen. The Golf, the Passat, and the Polo were all his creations. Leiding spent no money on the Beetle, other than to tide Volkswagen over by the allocation of a handful of coppers to keep it legal. The car he had been brought up on was of no use to him. The car that made him the executive he was had been ruined

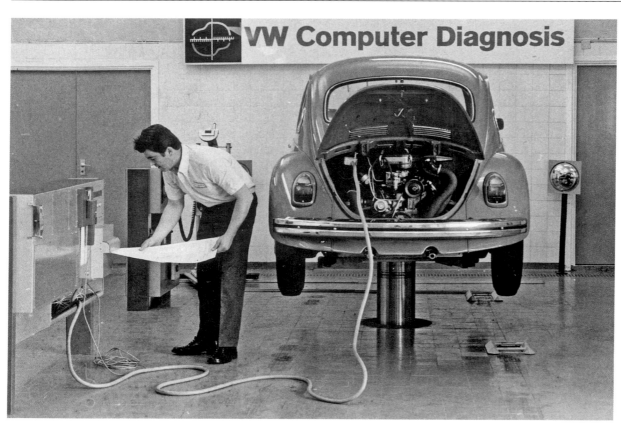

by his predecessor. There could be no turning back.

Rudolph Leiding was a Volkswagen man through and through. His career had blossomed under the great Heinz Nordhoff and by 1958, when his first really big opportunity arose, he was head of the service department. Nordhoff sent him to the Kassel plant as its head and several years later, in 1965, he was transferred to Auto Union. Here he galvanised into action the newly acquired division of the expanding Volkswagen empire, before setting sail for Brazil, again under Nordhoff's orders, with the challenge of reversing an alarming decline in Volkswagen's fortunes there. Nordhoff couldn't and wouldn't accept that a one-time 80 per cent market stranglehold had slipped to a derisory 66 per cent. Leiding reversed that trend almost at a stroke and, trouble shooter that he had become, hurried back to Audi-NSU to crack open and resolve a crucial unit cost issue. From such lofty pinnacles he headed to Wolfsburg as the third director general of Volkswagen and the only direct successor in the mould of Nordhoff.

Above: Servicing brought into a modern age – but the experiment was short-lived! Volkswagen's press release of September 1971 announced the innovation: 'Volkswagen's revolutionary Computer Diagnosis system is a more efficient, speedy and accurate method of checking a car's mechanical and electrical functions. The operator plugs in the VW, presses a button, and the computer prints out detailed information on the car's "state of health".'

Right: The 1972 model year saw not only the number of engine lid louvres increase from 10 to 26 but also what would prove to be a further increase in the size of the rear window – on this, the final occasion, by a further 40mm into the roof area.

Left and below: A sad day indeed as the very last Beetle to be built at Wolfsburg left the assembly line to make way for production of the Mk1 Golf. 11,916,519 Beetles had been built at Wolfsburg in the 29 years between 1945 and 1974.

Above: Inside, the Beetle was becoming more luxurious. This press image of the 1303's interior more or less hides the plastic dash, although the four-spoke safety steering wheel introduced for the '72 model year is clearly visible.

Right: To ensure compliance with anticipated American safety legislation, the 1302 Beetle developed into the 1303 – the curved-screen, moulded plastic dashboard model that many purists rejected as being un-Beetle like.

Leiding assumed the helm of the ailing giant on 1 October 1971 and immediately put a stop to the various haphazard and seemingly half-baked development programmes thrown together to replace the Beetle, and simmering into sogginess in Lotz's lukewarm cauldron. In their place a radical programme was initiated affecting every model in the Volkswagen range, with the possible exception of the Transporter. Leiding used technology and models developed by Audi and employed external design expertise; no stone was left unturned. As a result the first of an entirely different generation of Volkswagens went into production in just 18 months. This was the Passat, a close relation to the Audi 80 of the day, and the replacement for the VW 1600. Next came the Scirocco in March 1974 – a sporty coupé that some suggest was intended to replace the Karmann Ghia – and, close on its heels just two months later, the car Volkswagen had been waiting for, the intended Beetle successor, the Golf.

At 11:19am on 1 July 1974 the very last Beetle to be built at Wolfsburg, car number 11,916,519, rolled off the assembly line; European market production was transferred to Emden, where US-bound Beetles had been assembled since 1964. Wolfsburg, the factory built for the car that was originally the only Volkswagen, and the place where an unbroken production run of 30 years had occurred, no longer played a significant part in what would amount to almost a further three decades of manufacture, although bodyshells continued to be stamped out on the famous presses for a time.

Perhaps production of a smaller Volkswagen, the Polo – essentially a rebadged Audi 50, a car that emerged after Leiding's premature departure but which was most certainly of his making – serves as an indicator of the trouble and strife that beset the motor industry in general from 1973 onwards. Recurrent oil crises sounded a potential death knell for any gas guzzlers in a manufacturer's range, and in Volkswagen's case put paid to the already struggling VW 412; while roaring inflation unaccompanied by a parallel rise in wages ensured that all cars, whatever their nature, were considerably more expensive and less affordable. The smaller Polo carried a more palatable price-ticket than that of the Golf, one geared more closely to the budget of someone who in the past would have bought a Beetle.

The mid-1970s were challenging, survival-threatening times for all automobile manufacturers and many other

industries too. The recession was global in nature and exports declined for everyone, some companies seeing their sales figures tumble by as much as 40 per cent. Rampant inflation coupled to a volatile currency market ensured that even with a succession of price increases manufacturers' margins were shaved to dangerous levels. These were the problems Leiding had to contend with. That he had new models either completely ready for launch, or at a stage where light could already be seen at the end of the tunnel, was extremely fortunate. Sales of the Transporter, the only model in Volkswagen's range not due for imminent replacement, dropped from 294,932 examples built in 1972 to 289,022 the following year, followed by an alarming downward spiral to just 222,233 in 1974. Drops of this nature, amounting to close on 25 per cent, couldn't be sustained on an ongoing basis. Beetle output similarly went down, from 1,220,686 in 1972 to 1,206,018 the following year, and a catastrophic 791,053 in 1974. If it hadn't been for the presence of the Golf waiting in the wings this spectacular plummet of 35 per cent in 24 months could have driven Volkswagen to the wall.

Above: Wolfsburg continued to issue press images of the Beetle assembly line even as late as 1973, a year when production had started to decline slightly, albeit that 1,206,016 such cars were still produced worldwide.

Left: A publicity image released by Volkswagen of America depicts both the Super Beetle and the more basic torsion-bar car of 1974. Both were fitted with a 1600 engine, and apart from the large US market-only indicators also featured much sturdier bumpers than European examples.

Beetles of the Leiding era: the 1303 and special models

Possibly Rudolph Leiding's one act of kindness towards the Beetle was to allow Lotz's questionable spending to retain the US market's business to reach fruition. The 1303 Beetle was launched in the summer of 1972, just ten months after Leiding had ascended to the top job at Wolfsburg. Essentially, as has already been suggested, the latest Beetle was nothing more than a 1302 model with a radically curved windscreen, an all-new and distinctly plastic dashboard, and enormous rear-light clusters, which were of such gargantuan proportions that they quickly acquired the nickname of 'the elephant's foot'. There was no new engine; no alteration to the Lotz-era formula.

The undoubted external hallmark of the 1303 was its windscreen. Such was its design that it stood a full 42 per cent bigger than the largest of the so-called flat screens of other models. Some even suggested that the 1303 should be known as the 'Panorama' Beetle, and certainly its conservatory-style nature improved both forward vision and the car's aerodynamics. For the technocrats, the boot lid had to be clipped a little in length while the roof panel was elongated; an increase in the size of the windscreen wipers and blades was inevitable.

To accommodate the new tail-light clusters the rear wings had to be reshaped, making them both more rounded and slightly obese; a fitting match for the front wings introduced on the 1302 a couple of years earlier.

Inside the 1303 the new all-plastic health and safety-conscious dashboard, capable of deforming on impact, was undoubtedly the scourge of the purists, although – despite the mass of plastic – it was conservative in the wildness of the design mouldings compared to the offerings from the stables of other manufacturers, and was similarly austere in attendant instrumentation as it retained the traditional Beetle 'one dial for all purposes' philosophy. But it just wasn't befitting of a Beetle in many people's eyes. Fresh air vents with directional flaps sat

within a raised moulded section around the perimeter of the dashboard closest to the windscreen and offered better ventilation than previously, but Beetle purists were not impressed, as a quarter-light could always be opened if the vehicle began to steam up. Likewise, a raised and moulded shroud above the speedometer gained few accolades, and most failed to see the advantages of new-style rocker switches and their suggested easier accessibility. Few thought it beneficial for the glove-box to be compartmentalised, particularly if it was no longer possible to stand a drink or place a sandwich on the lid. Then there was a matter of taste: the centre strip of the dashboard was finished in black as standard, but for some special edition models, more of which shortly, this section was overlaid with a mock wood trim.

The 1303 in reality proved a mixed blessing. It did nothing to improve sales, and might even have contributed to the fall they experienced at about this time.

However, it had one worthwhile effect, as for the first time in many years the hood of the Cabriolet looked as though it was intended to connect with and flow seamlessly into the body of the car.

Essentials to meet legislation

Just as Leiding found the time to unpack his bags so new and tougher Californian emissions laws came into place – rules and regulations which would soon be extended to other states demanded that US cars be fitted with fuel injection. Bosch's design, although relatively simple and effective, centring on a fuel loop that supplied the injectors with fuel at constant pressure while the injectors were activated by contact points in the distributor, had little effect on performance or fuel economy. An inhibiting catalytic converter was part of the specification for California-bound cars of August 1974 vintage or later, while all other US Beetles had to be similarly equipped from the start of the 1977 model year.

Opposite and above: The day had finally arrived – 17 February 1972, the occasion of Beetle production exceeding that of the Model T Ford. Although director general Rudolph Leiding made the right noises it was nevertheless a day tinged with some sadness, as all those present knew that plans were in hand to replace Der Weltmeister. The assembly worker in the picture above holds a model of Ford's car, which was produced between 1908 and 1927.

Above: The 10-spoke pressed steel wheel manufactured by Lemmertz for Volkswagen's Der Weltmeister. Sprayed silver with a black centre section, the wheel's attractive appearance was enhanced by a polished alloy centre cap stamped with the VW roundel, and 19mm grey plastic wheel nut covers.

Above: Produced on heavy duty board, the certificate presented to the 1,500 lucky owners of British market World Champion 1300 Beetles included the celebratory medal, which was inlaid for its safekeeping (the wooden frame is an addition to what Volkswagen provided).

Below: 50mm diameter medallion to attach to the dashboard if so desired.

While the car photographed is a special edition model, it is also represents torsion bar Beetles produced from August 1967 onwards at the start of the '68 model year. Such cars, which bore a more determined stance than those of earlier models, featured vertically set headlamps, 'U'-section Europa bumpers, shorter boot and engine compartment lids and reshaped front and rear valances.

Right: The size of the Beetle's rear window increased every few years, the last change occurring on 1 August 1971 for the '72 model year and amounting to an additional 40mm in height as pictured. Similarly the number of cooling louvres in the engine lid was increased from 10 in two banks of five to 26 in total, banked in four unequal sets.

Below: From August 1967 all Beetles featured vertically set headlamps. (American market cars had benefited from the change 12 months earlier.)

Left: 1500 and 1300 Beetles built after August 1967 carried revised, larger rear light clusters. Later the design changed once more, but this style of lamp survived until August 1973. (Only 'L' specification cars featured the clear lens section for reversing lamps as standard. The owner of this Beetle added them as an £8.00 accessory when the car was bought!)

The World Champion Beetle could be distinguished externally from its contemporaries in three ways, two of which were instantly recognisable, the other less apparent. At the time the Marathon Blue metallic paintwork was unique to the special edition, while the Lemmertz sports wheels would remain forever exclusive to this celebratory model. The rubber bumper inserts are also visible in this picture.

Above: The style and more particularly the size of wing-mounted indicator pictured had been introduced in August 1963 and would remain current until the end of July 1973, when it was replaced by a bumper-mounted flasher (European markets – not USA).

Above: From the summer of 1967 and the introduction of the '68 model year Beetle, it was no longer necessary to lift the boot lid to gain access to the petrol tank filler cap. The cap was concealed behind the flap shown here. From August 1969 to the end of July 1972 this was opened by a lever inside the car, while in other years a finger release for the flap meant that a lockable petrol cap was a worthwhile purchase.

Above: Crescent-shaped through-flow air vents were an addition to the Beetle package for all models except the basic 1200 from August 1970. Two years later the bright-work trim was deleted, leaving a simple black plastic vent.

Below: The dashboard of this 1972 model year car is recognisable as being from the same stable of that of the 1959 car featured on pages 90–94. However, after evolving through various styles of steering wheel, from August 1971 the version pictured here became standard on all Beetles other than the 1200. Switches had become black instead of ivory coloured and were soft topped too. (Vinyl basket weave seat upholstery was the norm until the last years of Beetle production when increasing emphasis was placed on cloth.)

Right: The engine of the British market World Champion Beetle: the twin-port, 1285cc, 44PS unit known as the 1300. (Mainland Europe Weltmeisters based on the 1302S Beetle sported the 1584cc, 50PS engine.)

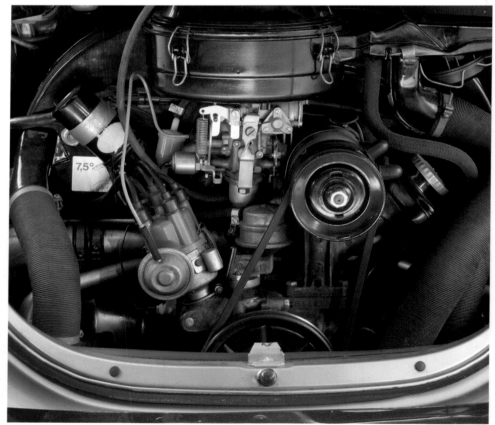

Special editions

A logical step for a manufacturer to take when sales tail off and a new model isn't ready for launch is to introduce special edition cars, vehicles that cost little more than the standard offering but come laden with additional trim and a name, or possibly a theme, which the marketing people can use to promote them. Despite continued growth in sales in the Lotz era, this tactic was employed with the Beetle from the early 1970s. Offerings initially included the June Beetle, a special devised to boost British sales, where the dealers were responsible for the addition of the component parts, which consisted entirely of items gathered from the

accessories cupboard. The largely but not exclusively US-orientated Super Vee was similar, regarding which stories abound of at least one British dealer selling the necessary bits in later years for more such models to be created by eager fans. By 1974, when Beetle sales genuinely started to tumble, Volkswagen were in full swing, with cars featuring special wheels, upholstery unique to the model, bespoke paint colours, and a whole host of limited edition model names.

Two such cars worthy of mention are the celebratory edition produced at the point when the Beetle became the most-produced car in the history of the

automobile, and the limited edition model offered to UK buyers to coincide with imports having reached the 300,000 mark.

'Der Weltmeister', known as the 'The World Champion Beetle' in Britain and, for reasons unknown, as the Baja Bug in the United States, was largely, but not exclusively, based on the 1302S, then the top of the range saloon. Apart from its unique paint shade, Marathon Blue metallic, which led to the edition being often referred to as the Marathon Beetle, and was later incorporated into the standard range of colour options, this vehicle's main attribute was its special steel wheels, produced by Lemmertz,

Below: Der Weltmeister or the World Champion Beetle as offered to British market customers.

In 1927, when production of the Model T Ford finally ended over 15,000,000 of that same vehicle had been manufactured. This established a world record in motor car production.

In 1972, with production still in progress the Volkswagen Beetle established a new world record in motor car production.
15,007,033 was the recorded figure for the 17th February 1972. The Beetle is now World Champion.

This medallion has been minted to celebrate the Volkswagen Beetles World Record.
And this certificate records the fact that one of a limited fifteen hundred distinctive commemorative models released to the U.K. is in the possession of

Above: A most-produced car history lesson, VW size, with accompanying 'gold' medal to prove it!

which came complete with shiny alloy centre caps. Rubber bumper inserts in the style of 'L' models developed from the late 1960s onwards are hardly worthy of mention. A plethora of certificates, medallions, and booklets, all dedicated to reiterating the 'World Champion' message although worth little in monetary terms, boosted the exclusivity and collectability of the edition.

The British version of the World Champion Beetle was based on the torsion-bar 1300 model for reasons that are not entirely clear. 1,500 examples were trundled into the dealers' showrooms, which in reality meant that the main ones received six vehicles, while other agents were restricted to only three.

The GT Beetle, like the World Champion before it, sold very quickly, although in

this instance the unusual course was taken of producing a sales brochure to promote it. Offered in what were described as 'three fruity' colours – Tomato Red, Lemon Yellow, and Apple Green, all of which, most suggest, were standard paint shades with new names – the GT was based on a model not exported to Britain, the 1300S, a torsion-bar car with a 50PS engine and disc brakes at the front. Features which ensured that these cars were much sought after included steel sports wheels, soon to become a staple ingredient of limited-edition models; cloth upholstery, ahead of the general trend towards material rather than vinyl in Britain; the recently launched 1303's rear wings and large lamp clusters, again in advance of such items filtering through to all Beetles; and dealer-fitted goodies such as a sports gear shift, a tunnel tray, and a coveted GT Beetle badge on the engine lid. Best of all, the GT cost only £19 more than a standard 1300 model! The 300,000th Beetle to arrive on British shores did so in December 1972, and the edition of 2,500 cars was virtually sold out by March 1973.

Space precludes a description of all the special edition Beetles, but the desirability of those that follow demands that they should at least be mentioned, however briefly.

For Germany only, the 1973 Black and Yellow Racer was essentially a 1303S with Saturn Yellow paint, black bumpers, and black boot and engine lids, while the Sports Bug, of which 20,000 examples were sold, was essentially the same car but designed for the American market.

1974 to 1975 saw three runs of Jeans Beetles. As the name implies, these 1200-model specials were designed with the younger buyer in mind. Denim upholstery was matched with side decals, the by now obligatory sports wheels, and Tunis Yellow paint. In total it is estimated that over 50,000 such cars were sold.

The Big Beetle, also of 1974 vintage, was based on the 1303S and came with side stripes, a dashboard wood-effect centre strip, both a sports steering wheel and gear shift, what the marketing pundits described as 'fat radial tyres', and $5\frac{1}{2}$J 'Rally' wheels.

Right: Hardly the steamiest of brochures to promote the hottest of Beetles – its four pages had just one dash of colour across its centre spread.

The GT Beetle:
A very special Beetle at a very special price.

Across the pond, La Grande Bug was almost a photocopy of the European Big Beetle but, in a land where sunshine is plentiful, included a sunroof.

A cascade of European specials followed, with the Herringbone or 1200 Super, which arrived in 1974 but lingered into 1975; the 1303 Campaign with its gorgeous chocolate brown metallic paint; and the Sun Beetle, which, as might be anticipated, came with a sunroof.

Similarly, in the United States, where there seemed to be considerable panic concerning the Beetle's ability to last the course, there came the Luxury Bug and the Sun Bug, neither of whose designations require much stretch of the imagination to guess their make-up. As for the Love Bug, Disney and the lovable Herbie came to the rescue!

A fitting way to close this whirlwind charge through the glitter and tinsel of the Beetle's closing years as a German-built wonder is to turn to Volkswagen's American Press Office and quote from their release for the '76 model year:

'The 1976 Beetle, now on display at area VW dealerships, comes with so many luxury "extras" included as standard equipment that it may still be the best automotive bargain on the market today. Among the features VW includes as standard are fuel injection, wall-to-wall carpeting, metallic paint, an electric window defogger, front vent windows and sports wheel rims...'

Left: The image reproduced here is of a forerunner of the sought-after Jeans Beetle, one of the most popular of all such cars. Perhaps the decidedly authentic body stitching was deemed one step too far, as the production Jeans Beetle lacked this startling attribute.

Left: Special editions proliferated as the 1970s gathered pace and the Beetle's future looked increasingly insecure. The 1976 US-market Luxury Bug featured, amongst other things, frequently specified steel sports wheels, mock wood dashboard inserts, 'wall-to-wall' carpeting, and an 'electric rear window defogger'.

Far left and left: At long last, for the '74 model year the 1200 Beetle received a makeover. Apart from its own style of matt black Europa bumpers complete with silver centre tape, the base model adopted the recently introduced tail lights of the 1303 model on appropriately reshaped rear wings. The car in the pictures dates from 1975, by which time hubcaps had been deleted in favour of plastic wheel nut and centre covers.

1975 and a sign of the times: seven water-cooled cars overshadowed the Beetle range, which at least as far as this picture was concerned comprised the basic 1200 (second row left), a 1303 (second row right), and at the front a 1200L to the right and the Cabriolet to the left. Beetle production that year dwindled to 441,116 cars.

Slimming the range

Once the Golf and its water-cooled brethren had not only been launched but were seen to be selling in showrooms across the Volkswagen empire, the company was confident enough to hack back the now extensive Beetle range. With the sole exception of the Cabriolet the axe came for all elements of the 1303 line at the end of July 1975, as it did for torsion-bar 1300 models. For the start of the 1976 model year in August 1975, the range shrivelled to no more than a 34PS saloon in basic or more commonly De Luxe format, for a select few a 1600 engine version of the 'L' model, and the 1303-based Cabriolet. Cynics decried Volkswagen's actions, citing such an underpowered 34PS-dominated remnant of the range as a deliberate attempt by the company to depress Beetle sales further. If that was genuinely Volkswagen's intention it certainly worked. Production plunged downwards from a depressing 791,053 cars worldwide in 1974

Above and left: With the Golf successfully launched for the '76 model year the Beetle range was hacked back to just one torsion-bar model – the everlasting 1200. Widely available in De Luxe or 'L' guise, as illustrated here, the home market also benefited from a basic 1200, while some markets could order a 1200LS, a De Luxe 1200 with the 50PS 1600 engine.

to a dismal 441,116 in 1975, an even more miserable 383,277 units the following year, and so on. In reality, satellite factories were assembling – or in Latin America manufacturing – the lion's share of Beetle annual production totals. Beetle sales in the USA tumbled to 82,030 in 1975, whilst in Germany, where 323,513 units had been registered in 1970, the figure was no more than 41,070, a gigantic drop from the previous year's 118,915 vehicles and one set to plummet even further, to just 6,524 in 1977. The inevitable was forecast with monotonous frequency.

The end of German production

At midday on 19 January 1978 the last Beetle saloon ever to be manufactured on German soil tumbled off the Emden assembly line. The basic 1200, which, considering the historic nature of the event and the attention the occasion would create, amazingly lacked all elements of its final trim, bore the chassis number 118 2 034 030, and represented the 16,255,500th such car to be built in the Fatherland since the war. Total worldwide production at that point had reached 19,300,000. A resurgence in Cabriolet sales – no doubt brought about by persistent rumours of the car's demise – ensured survival for a further two years until a similarly topless Golf could be given sufficient rigidity to take its place.

For director general Toni Schmücker and the rest of the Volkswagen management team the life of the Beetle had run its course and its value was exhausted. Pandering to the whims of a few dedicated, diehard enthusiasts they nevertheless sought assistance from the Mexican factory and imported Beetles from Puebla; a device intended to run for a very short time until any furore had extinguished itself. Little did anyone realise that the Beetle would still be available in one location or another for a further quarter of a century.

Below and opposite: The Cabriolet outlived the German-built Beetle by two years, production eventually coming to an end in January 1980. When rumours of the Cabriolet's demise in favour of a Golf soft-top emerged, sales escalated – particularly so in the USA.

The essentially bespoke Cabriolet was always
regarded as being at the top of the Beetle range,
its price, if nothing else, demanding such a status.
While the 1303 curved screen saloon was much
criticised by the diehards as the most un-Beetle-
like of Beetles, in Cabriolet form the car was both
popular and more aesthetically pleasing than some
of the earlier soft-top applications. All Cabriolets
were assembled for Volkswagen by the coachbuilders
Karmann and their insignia was duly attached to
the front quarter-panel of the car.

Above: Although still small by the standards of water-cooled Volkswagens, the 1302 and 1303's boot was positively cavernous compared to that of the torsion bar cars. This was in part due to the spare wheel being laid flat below the lower section of the boot. The petrol tank was the principal cause of the boot being split into a lower and higher section. The windscreen washer bottle was located in the boot of all Beetles from the date of its introduction in the 1960s.

Below: The dashboard of the curved screen 1303 would have looked at home in many a car of the 1970s, German or otherwise. However despite the relatively conservative nature of the design, to many a would-be Beetle purchaser and to the vast majority of enthusiasts the dashboard was totally unsuited to the car. After all, it was no longer possible to place a picnic cup on the opened glove-box lid, while a hooded gauge was far too modern!

Above: The introduction of the 1303 Beetle saw the arrival of the largest rear light cluster to be offered on the Beetle; a fitting that would remain standard to the end of Beetle production in Mexico in 2003. Due to its proportions and shape, enthusiasts named this style of rear light cluster the elephant's foot.

Above: No German-built Beetle had alloys incorporated into the specification, but during the 1970s the steel sports wheel became increasingly the norm for special models, of which the Cabriolet might be considered a member in the loosest sense.

Right and below: Throughout its lengthy production run the Beetle Cabriolet's hood remained a masterpiece of the coachbuilder's craft, incorporating several layers of insulating material and, most unusually when compared to far more expensive contemporaries, relying on glass rather than Perspex for the rear window. Note how beautifully the hood met the specially created chromed side window frames, both of which could be wound down when the hood was in fresh air mode.

Far left: The secret of the Cabriolet's relative rigidity despite its lack of a roof was in the strengthening of various areas of the car. This image illustrates the measures taken to make the inner sills more robust.

Left: The interior of the later 1970s cars was relatively luxurious, as had always been the case in an unadorned sort of way. Whereas later saloons would benefit from cloth upholstery, Cabriolet Beetles retained vinyl, which was a sensible move when the hood was down and rain threatened!

Opposite: The frontal stance of both the 1302 and 1303 Beetles, the cars with MacPherson strut suspension, was totally different to that of other Beetles, the torsion bar models. The somewhat bloated appearance of the boot lid and the wider, possibly fatter-looking, wings, led some critics to describe such cars as 'pregnant Beetles'.

Left: Once the twin-port 1600 engine had been introduced virtually all Cabriolets were endowed with the 50PS power-plant, just as their owners had previously enjoyed the benefits of the largest available engine since the days when the 1300 made its debut.

1978-2003 MEXICAN AND BRAZILIAN BEETLES

Nordhoff's prediction, made a few weeks before his death, that the Beetle's star would continue to shine brightly for many years to come, was destined to become true, for after German production had come to an end it would continue to thrive in Latin America, retaining its core value as a car for the people, and sought after by the people, easily passing the 20-million milestone that Lotz had decreed with such certainty would never be reached.

Revised Beetle boundaries

At the point Beetle production ceased in Germany the number of factories assembling or building Beetles was already on the decline. When Nordhoff died nearly ten years previously expansion was still a reality, while the reaction of the satellite bodies to Lotz's inept pronouncements was generally one of a determination to forge ahead, whatever Wolfsburg was doing. However, in the space of a few short years all had changed across large parts of the globe. Australian interest had evaporated by 1976 and with it the lingering hopes of one-time assemblers in New Zealand, whose last cars emerged in 1972. Thailand, Singapore, Malaysia, and Indonesian interests had gone one by one, the last-mentioned as recently as 1977, leaving the Philippines as the sole Far East country still assembling Beetles, something they would continue to do until 1986.

Closer to home, and certainly more directly entangled in Wolfsburg's tentacles, Belgian manufacture ceased in 1975 and Portuguese assembly came to a permanent halt in 1976, as did the activities of the company's Yugoslavian outpost. Southern Irish interests faded away in 1977 after a

Right: South African Beetle production ground to a halt in 1979, but just a year earlier the factory was manufacturing versions of the 1303 and 1300. A quick glance at the images reveals that variations existed between the specifications of South African cars and German-built Beetles. The older Beetle in the picture, with the Uitenhage plant in the background, was believed to be the oldest Volkswagen resident in South Africa and dated from 1949.

run spanning 27 years, while the South African factory at Uitenhage closed its doors on Beetle manufacture for the last time in 1979 with a suitably exclusive and lavishly trimmed model.

Despite this apparent global retraction, the Beetle thrived in South America in the hands of two of its most devoted followers. Mexico's love affair with the car variously nicknamed *El Escarabajo* (Scarab Beetle) or *El Vocho* (Little Child) began in 1954, while its overwhelming presence in Brazil, where its name translated to *Fusca*, extended to a number of operations that built Beetles from parts supplied by the São Paulo factory. These included Venezuela (1963–81), Uruguay (1961–82), Peru (1966–87), far-flung Nigeria (1975–89), and already mentioned Manila in the Philippines, where Brazil took over in 1977 from where Wolfsburg left off. With the exception of Mexico, only one Latin American country escaped Brazil's tentacles and that was Costa Rica, which assembled Beetles between 1970 and 1975 from parts shipped in from Wolfsburg.

VW do Brasil

The awards showered on Nordhoff by the Brazilian people in his lifetime, including the freedom of the City of São Bernado do Campo, and the respect with which he was treated following his death (a period of official mourning was declared), serve to illustrate just how important Volkswagen, and by default the Beetle, was to the country. From inevitably humble beginnings, the Beetle had become Brazil's best-selling car, with over 30,000 units being purchased annually by 1962. Expansion continued apace and by 1966 Volkswagen employed 11,000 workers at its factory, turned out 95,000 vehicles annually, and accounted for 62 per cent of all cars sold in the country. It is no wonder, then, that on 4 July 1967 the 500,000th Fusca rolled off the São Paulo assembly line.

Brazil's faith in the Beetle remained constant long after Wolfsburg had questioned its very existence. Within less than five years of one celebration, a further production milestone demanded

another, for in March 1972 the millionth Beetle rolled off the assembly line. 223,453 Fuscas were sold that year, while a further 6,000 examples were exported. Within two years sales had increased to 237,323 cars, of which by this time nearly 24,500 were exported. By mid-1976 the 2,000,000th Brazilian Beetle had emerged, the satellite operations were in full swing, and, in the style of Wolfsburg in the Nordhoff era, the Fusca was finding a home in some 60 countries across the globe.

However, as the 1980s gathered pace interest in the Beetle declined and by 1984 home market sales had fallen to as few as 34,000 cars. What was assumed to be the last Fusca forever left the São Paulo assembly line on 7 December 1986, by which time total production numbers had reached in excess of 3,321,251 cars. Then, amazingly, the Beetle made an unprecedented return to production in August 1993, when six and a half years of dust had been allowed to gather on its elderly presses. The Brazilian President,

anxious not to lose the support of an emerging class of citizens for whom, for the first time, owning a motor car was no longer just a wishful dream, demanded that the government should avoid a damaging upsurge in cheap Japanese imports by allowing the state-funded car industry, Autolatina, to assist with the reintroduction of the home-built Beetle at a subsidised price. Once back in production at a rate of 200 cars per day it was discovered that older, more affluent people were also anxious to add a Beetle to their portfolio as a second car. Coupled with the Beetle's legendary ability to deal with rugged terrain in a country where outside the bigger conurbations road surfaces varied between appalling and non-existent, the Fusca's future once more looked bright. Sadly, however, a change in government policy just under three years later brought an end to the tax incentives that had made production feasible and on 11 July 1996 production ceased once more, this time forever.

Fusca.
As boas idéias são simples.

Left: The Brazilian Beetle of the 1990s, known as the Fusca.

A deviant Beetle

When director general Toni Schmücker decided that it was necessary to placate Beetle diehards by importing cars from Latin America after production at Emden ceased, it might have seemed logical that he should turn to the Beetle's Brazilian stronghold for assistance. However, this was not the case and never could have been. Global corporate policy had decreed that all technical developments and the majority of manufacturing production were to be carried out under the guiding hand and supervisory control of Wolfsburg. One major exception to this rule prevailed, and that was the Brazilian operation. While the South African factory might have to be sanctioned to produce the most unlikely of models, a 1303-bodied torsion-bar Beetle, in São Paulo the technicians had the necessary autonomy to go their own way.

As a result, slowly but surely the Fusca became a breed of Beetle independent of the rest. When, in 1965, Beetle windows were increased in size, Volkswagen do Brasil didn't follow suit and never would. Disc brakes, a progression granted to European 1500 models for the '67 model year, only became an option in Brazil in 1973, while dual circuit brakes debuted as late as 1978. Rear swing axles were never upgraded, but Europa-style bumpers of 1968 German model year fame filtered through to the Fusca in 1970. Between 1960 and 1973 Fusca wheels bore a similarity to those of a Porsche 356, offering ventilated, five-bolt, open centre rims. When a 1600 engine was introduced in 1976 it came with twin carburettors, while 14in wheels became standard. In 1978, the Brazilian Beetle adopted a unique style of steering wheel, while in a few years time it would acquire a padded dashboard with square-dial instruments. Significantly, alcohol-fuelled cars would play an increasingly significant part in the line-up of available models.

Hecho en Mexico

With VW do Brasil excluded as an appropriate candidate to take remaining Beetle sales forward in Europe, Schmücker turned to the altogether less significant Mexican operation. Importing origins dated back to 1954, but due to government intervention quickly turned to CKD assembly at the factory at Xalostoc, where local content of ever-increasing percentages ensued until 1966, when a new factory was opened at Puebla, some 78 miles from Mexico City. Full manufacture ensued, and while production never reached the lofty heights of either the German factories or even the Brazilian operation, they were dependable. In total 17,630 sedans were produced in 1967, by 1970 this figure had risen to 35,303, and by 1974 it had more than doubled again to 77,391. A severe decline followed – the result of one of Mexico's frequent financial crises – although by 1978, and with the stimulus of exports to mainland Europe, production had clawed its way back up to 51,697 cars.

*Right and below:
Immediately after
German Beetle
production ceased
forever Volkswagen
began to import Beetles
from Mexico. These
images show the South
American-built cars
being unloaded
at Emden.*

Although from the start of the period of outright manufacture there were variances between the German and Mexican-produced Beetles, these were more or less ironed out during the 1970s. Between 1968 and 1971 Mexican Beetles retained the German specification window sizes of cars produced before the '65 model year, and were also offered with both old-style kingpin front suspension and five-stud wheels complete with domed hubcaps of years gone by. However, vertical headlamps, Europa-style bumpers, and rear-light clusters of the style of the German 1500 and 1300 prevailed. After this date, though, the only significant external difference between a German torsion-bar car – Mexico never ventured into 1302 or 1303 territory – and a Mexican one was the size of the rear window, as Puebla failed to adopt the last size update of '72 model year vintage.

Left: Friday 15 May 1981 bore witness to the arrival of the 20-millionth Beetle to roll off Beetle assembly lines across the world. To mark the occasion a special limited edition Silver Bug became available.

The specification of the imported Mexican Beetles of 1978 centred upon the 34PS engine fitted with a DC generator rather than an AC alternator, radial tyres, and a full 'L' trim level, including a heated rear window and an anti-dazzle mirror, as well as adjustable head restraints. Omitted was the two-speed electric ventilation fan of recent Emden years, while the rear valance was flat, unlike those of cars produced in Germany from August 1974. Chrome tailpipes and brightwork running-board trim both made a return, while for 1200 models the addition of four banks of cooling louvres in the engine lid was unusual and a feature that would disappear on 30 July 1981.

The post-Emden Beetle *hecho en Mexico* made its way into various European countries, including Austria, Italy, and Switzerland, but wasn't an option for legislation-cocooned America, or right-hand-drive Britain. Sadly, the day would

come when the Beetle was forced out of Switzerland, a departure caused by noise pollution legislation in the grand American style. Nevertheless, if Germany one day was seen to falter, other European countries weren't. Puebla must have been jubilant to learn that in the year their 100,000th Beetle was exported European sales topped the 15,000 mark, even if Germany contributed no more than 5,000 of those new car registrations.

West Germans registered 10,876 Beetles in 1978, a 66 per cent increase on the previous year. 1979 saw a further advance, with 14,650 new Beetles being driven on German roads for the first time. From this high the figures tailed away to 6,271 vehicles in 1982, when a by now age-old answer to dipping sales was introduced in the form of a succession of special models, a move that bore fruit in the registration of 12,622 cars in 1983 and 11,061 the following year. Sadly,

a desultory 5,087 sales in 1985 decided Volkswagen's latest director general, one-time Nordhoff protégé and Beetle champion Carl Hahn, that an end must come. Perhaps not surprisingly Beetle registrations rocketed, particularly as the last edition model offered pundits a decidedly attractive package.

Mexican specials, like their German predecessors, had nothing to do with up-rated engines or mechanical components, and relied instead on distinctive paint shades and higher trim levels to boost sales. Perhaps the first such model should be discounted as being of this type as it was produced for another and very special reason, for on 15 May 1981 the 20-millionth Beetle emerged from the Puebla assembly line. The commemorative Silver Bug featured, as its name implies, silver metallic paint, decorative side stripes, a suitable decal on the engine lid, a special plaque incorporated into the gear knob

and, as an added bonus, an exclusive 20 million key-fob.

Spring 1982 saw the Jeans Beetle reborn, albeit in more lavish guise, while in the autumn of the same year the Special Bug arrived. This model was available in either Mars Red or Metallic Black and stood out from the crowd thanks to virtually every conceivable part being finished in black, which in turn was complemented by gold side-stripes and a similar decal on the engine lid. From here special Beetles were commonplace. The 2,000 run Aubergine Beetle went on sale in the spring of 1983, soon to be followed by the first of two editions of the Winter Beetle, an Ice Blue metallic car with matching upholstery, shiny wheel trims and more. In total 3,800 examples of this popular special were sold. The Sunny Bug was most notable not for its striking yellow paintwork, but for its lurid orange-yellow cloth upholstery, although to many people's surprise all 1,800 examples cleared quite quickly. In contrast the Velvet Red Beetle, a mid-1984 introduction of which 2,400 were produced, featured particularly attractive red-and-blue striped velour upholstery, a perfect complement to its red paintwork with surprisingly understated blue flower decals on its sides.

The final edition to be sold in Germany and elsewhere on European soil was commonly known as the Jubilee Beetle. 3,150 such cars were brought in during August 1985, the 50th anniversary of Porsche's first Beetle prototype, and all were finished in 'Zinngraue Metallic' with a '50 Jahre Käfer' decal on both the engine lid and left front quarter-panel, complementary silver side-stripes, meaty sports wheels boasting 165 SR15 tyres, green-tinted heat-resistant glass, and an interior of the utmost taste. Soft grey upholstery discreetly enhanced by subtle red and grey centre stripes blended well with carefully matched grey trim panels and carpets. A steering wheel virtually identical to that fitted to the second generation Golf of the era was a considerable improvement over the rather dated style of wheel which dated back to 1972, but was still prevalent on all other Beetles 13 years later.

Above: The limited edition Silver Bug, produced to celebrate production of the 20-millionth Beetle, with Metallic Silver paintwork and black lower body side-stripes etched with the words 'Silver Bug'. The gear lever carried a suitable commemorative disc.

Right: The 20-millionth Beetle with Volkswagen's fellow museum resident – the 1938 KdF-Wagen.

Continual improvement – Mexican style

Many would have anticipated that if former director general Rudolph Leiding was asked to speak of the Mexican Beetle he would condemn it out of hand. But Leiding was no Lotz, and even many years after his departure from Volkswagen he could see merit in the old master for certain markets. 'It is undeniable that for Mexico the Beetle was the ideal automobile. In this country, where the paved roads ended and other models failed, the Beetle kept right on going towards its goal ... in this market the Beetle had displaced its competitors.'

As an echo of the age of Nordhoff, the Mexican Beetle developed over the 18-year period following the cessation of exports to Europe until its final demise in 2003 in the same way it had in Germany in the 1950s and 1960s. One cloud only lay on the horizon of an otherwise blue sky. Unlike Nordhoff's Germany, where the economy blossomed for much of his tenure in office, Mexico's financial stability, or rather the lack of it, had the power to bring the Beetle crashing down when it least expected to.

Playing its part to the full, Puebla updated the Beetle in anticipation of customers' requirements, offering two levels of trim, best summarised as basic and De Luxe, or Sedan and Sedan GL, latterly City and Classic, both of which were based on one power unit. Particularly attractive special edition models that kept the Beetle at the forefront of the minds of Mexican citizens included both the 'Car of the Century' and Wolfsburg editions of October 1991 vintage, the '40 years' (of Mexican production), the Fire Beetle and yet another Jeans model which were issued in 1994, and the Celebration model which followed 12 months later.

From such simple upgrades as those offered for 1987 model year cars, when the headlining became blue rather than white (although two years hence it would change again to soft grey) and the wipers were offered with an intermittent wash-wipe facility, to a new-style steering wheel and the discontinuation of the somewhat antiquated passenger footrest two years later, luxuries and aesthetics were never overlooked. Replicating the general trend to abandon chrome and other brightwork, the boot lid became plain in the latter part of 1992, while in 1995 the Beetle's already upgraded, wider than previously, bumpers became body colour-coded, as did the headlamp trims. At the same time in-vogue black replaced chrome or aluminium on such items as the door handles, front side window surrounds, and even the front lid-mounted VW roundel. Waistline trim, for so many years of polished aluminium, first became black and then, in October 1995, was deleted altogether. Hubcaps were set to be spray-painted rather than chromed and by 1997 even the VW roundel had been dispensed with.

Of greater significance, however, were the advances made by the introduction of electronic ignition in 1988 on a by now standard 1600 engine, the application of dual circuit brakes from October 1991, and, most significantly of all for the Beetle, the introduction of Digifant fuel injection in all cars just a year later in October 1992. In 1994 front disc brakes replaced less effective drums, while the 5J x 15 steel wheels were by now fitted with 155 SR 15 radial tyres.

By the mid-1990s, the 1600i (as the product was now branded) offered maximum power of 44PS at 4,000rpm from its fuel-injected, catalytic converter-suppressed 1,584cc engine. Compression ratio was 7.7:1 and maximum torque stood at 94Nm at 2,200rpm.

Below: The 20-millionth Beetle with another legend in motoring history, the Ford Model T.

Above: A spate of special-edition Beetles were designed to augment sales to the diehards in Germany and other selected European countries in the 1980s, at a time when the Golf already reigned supreme. This model is the Winter Bug, a car that was always finished in Ice Blue metallic paint.

Above right: The last batch of Beetles to be imported from Mexico for sale in Europe coincided with the 50th anniversary of the assembly of the first prototypes.

Right: Sometimes a little meaning can be lost in translation: '17 Oktober 1985 – 50 Jahre Käfer. Ein Symbol hat Jubiläum'; '17 octobre 1985 – 50ans Coccinelles. Le jubilée d'un symbole'; '17 October 1985 – 50 years Beetle. Jubilee for a symbol.'

Fuel injection not only offered exceptionally smooth running but also boosted fuel economy, with only the heaviest-footed being incapable of achieving at least 40mpg. Acceleration from 0–60mph in 17 seconds was somewhat leisurely, but a top speed of 95mph was more than acceptable.

Última Edición

That the specification of the Última Edición Beetle was fitting is without question. Combining the latest developments in Beetle technology in 21st-century guise with a genuinely retro feel was a masterstroke. The 3,000 cars were finished in either Aquarius Blue or Harvest Moon Beige, shades reminiscent of some of the most popular hues of the 1950s and 1960s, but nevertheless thoroughly modern in their appeal and popular options for the contemporary Puebla-built New Beetle. Complementing the paintwork was a rekindled package of chrome and brightwork trim, a shiny extravaganza of the former that extended from the bumpers and hubcaps to the door handles, boot and engine lid catches, and a highly buffed side salad of anodised aluminium in the form of running board, boot lid and waistline strips. Whitewall tyres, so commonplace several decades previously, and particularly so in the United States, formed another vital part of the specification, but the crowning glory had to be the rebirth of the much sought-after Wolfsburg Crest boot lid badge, a feature of De Luxe Beetles built after April 1951 and

Production numbers

From a low of just 16,746 cars built in 1986 (the year following the demise of exports), production bounced back, the biggest leap of all coming between 1989, a year when a significant 32,421 Sedans were built, to 1990, when for the first time in the history of Mexican manufacture over 80,000 Beetles (84,716 to be precise) were built in a 12-month period. Nor was this a one-year wonder, as for the next four years similarly joyful figures were achieved. Puebla revelled in the production of the 21-millionth Beetle on 23 June 1992, before the peak in production came in 1993, when an astonishing 98,236 cars left the factory.

Sadly, economic depression and accompanying drastic devaluations of the peso left production stunted in 1994 when just 15,933 Beetles were produced. However, by the turn of the century Beetle sales amounted to a healthy 41,260 cars and once again the future looked rosy. A total of 38,850 cars was more than acceptable in 2001; the drop to 24,007 in 2002, however, was of some concern. However, when by the middle of 2003 only just over 7,500 Beetles had been built and legislation had come into force banning the Beetle as a vehicle appropriate for use as a taxi, most were aware that the time had finally come for the car to bid farewell.

On Thursday 10 July 2003 Dr Jens Neumann, a member of the management board of Volkswagen AG, announced that production would end very shortly. 3,000 Ultimate Edition Beetles went into production with immediate effect. On Wednesday 30 July car number 21,529,464 – the very last Beetle ever to be manufactured, an Aquarius Blue Última Edición – left the Puebla assembly line destined for Wolfsburg and a place of honour in the company's archive of landmark cars. Although demand had finally faltered there was no reason for its followers to hang their heads in shame. As Neumann said in his valedictory address, 'True stars, and their fans, know when it's time to quit.'

Left: Mexico's 1988 model year Sedan bore a great visual similarity to German Beetles of a decade earlier. Under the skin, though, changes were taking place. Modifications suited to the Mexican market now predominated.

in this instance reproduced in the style of the version adorning such cars from August 1959 through to October 1962.

Inside the final models were as modern as any Beetle could be and even incorporated a radio/CD player and four speakers, although one retro styling feature did exist. While padded dashboards had been a feature of Mexican Beetles for over 25 years, the decision to paint the glove-box lid and the grilles surrounding the single dial in the car's body-colour was highly reminiscent of 'L' specification Beetles of the late 1960s when such a luxury was first introduced.

The enormity of the Beetle success story

21,529,464 Beetles were built in a continuous production run spanning the years 1945 to 2003. Compare this figure with the total production number of some of the West's best-loved and never to be forgotten motoring icons and the enormity of the achievement is clear to see. Fiat's delightful little 500, so recently reincarnated, but originally spanning the years 1957 to 1975, weighed in at 3,678,000 vehicles sold, only to be overtaken by the cleverly packaged but largely forgotten

Below: The 1993 model year Mexican Sedan 1600i.

Right: A publicity image depicting the 2001 model year Beetle.

Far right: Beetle assembly at Volkswagen's Puebla plant in the 21st century.

127 (1971–83) with a total of 3,779,086 sales. Citroën's 2CV, with a production run spanning from 1949 to 1990, encompassed 3,868,634 saloons and an additional 1,246,335 vans, a grand total of 5,114,969 vehicles. Britain's beloved Mini teetered a little above such lofty heights at 5,378,776 cars of all types sold between 1959 and 2000, but the earlier and equally treasured Morris Minor, or from 1956 Morris 1000, amassed no more than 1,293,331 units between 1948 and 1971. Heading the field of European contenders is the Renault 4, another symbol of French determination and a car that saw a continuous production run of 31 years between 1961 and 1992, during which time 8,135,424 were built. Way out ahead, of course, was the Ford Model T, which was the car

that the Beetle had to overtake to gain its *Weltmeister* status. At the time Volkswagen thought they had a stunning total of 15,007,033 to beat, and duly claimed the title when this figure was passed. Inevitably, somewhere in their own dank and dusty archives Ford found evidence of a few more cars, but nothing that came even close to the additional millions needed to keep up with the Beetle. Not that the achievements of Ford and other US manufacturers should be belittled – they were eminently capable of producing big quantities in generally short spaces of time, with Ford's Model A, for example, amassing a total of 3,562,610 cars in just four years between 1927 and 1931.

This, then, has been the story of the Beetle, the most produced car of all time, a

record that it will in all likelihood hold in perpetuity. From Porsche and his unholy alliance with Hitler, through the years of the British and Ivan Hirst's improvisation, the Beetle's creation and survival was little short of a miracle. Then, after 20 years of sound business sense and unprecedented success under its unwavering mentor, the Beetle should have once again withered and died, its vital arteries slowly but surely severed one by one by bumbling Lotz and ruthless Leiding. Instead, it survived and prospered in lands suited to it and it to them. From first prototype in 1935 to the early years of the 21st century, a remarkable journey of 68 years in total, the Beetle stood triumphant, no adversary having sufficient ethereal power to hasten its demise.

Left and bottom left: The last Beetle, an Aquarius Blue Última Edición, left the production line at Puebla at 9:05am on Wednesday 30 July 2003, number 21,529,464, in a direct manufacturing line going back to the days and months after the Second World War.

Below: The centre spread from the brochure produced to promote the Última Edición.

This spread: The 3,000 cars that formed the Última Edición were available in either Aquarius Blue or Luna Beige. Trim details included a once-only return of the Wolfsburg Crest bonnet badge and the old American favourite of whitewall tyres. A result of many years of continual improvement in Mexico, just as had been the case in Germany during Nordhoff's 20 years at the helm, the Última Edición is a car that the Beetle's greatest protagonist would have been happy to call his own.

INDEX